CH

Recentering the Universe

Recentering the Universe

The Radical Theories of Copernicus, Kepler, Galileo, and Newton

RON MILLER

TWENTY-FIRST CENTURY BOOKS / MINNEAPOLIS

This book is for Tom Miller.

Twenty-First Century Books
A division of Lerner Publishing Group, Inc.
241 First Avenue North
Minneapolis, MN 55401 USA

For reading levels and more information, look up this title at www.lernerbooks.com.

Main body text set in Gama ITC Std Book 11/15.
Typeface provided by International Typeface Corp.

Library of Congress Cataloging-in-Publication Data

Miller, Ron, 1947—
    Recentering the universe : the radical theories of Copernicus, Kepler, Galileo, and Newton / by Ron Miller.
        p.   cm.
    Includes bibliographical references and index.
    ISBN 978-0-7613-5885-5 (lib. bdg. : alk. paper)
    ISBN 978-0-7613-1662-8 (eBook)
    1. Astronomy—History—Juvenile literature. 2. Astronomy—Religious aspects—Christianity—History—Juvenile literature. I. Title.
QB15.M53 2014
523.1—dc23   2012047665

Manufactured in the United States of America
2 - BP - 11/1/13

CONTENTS

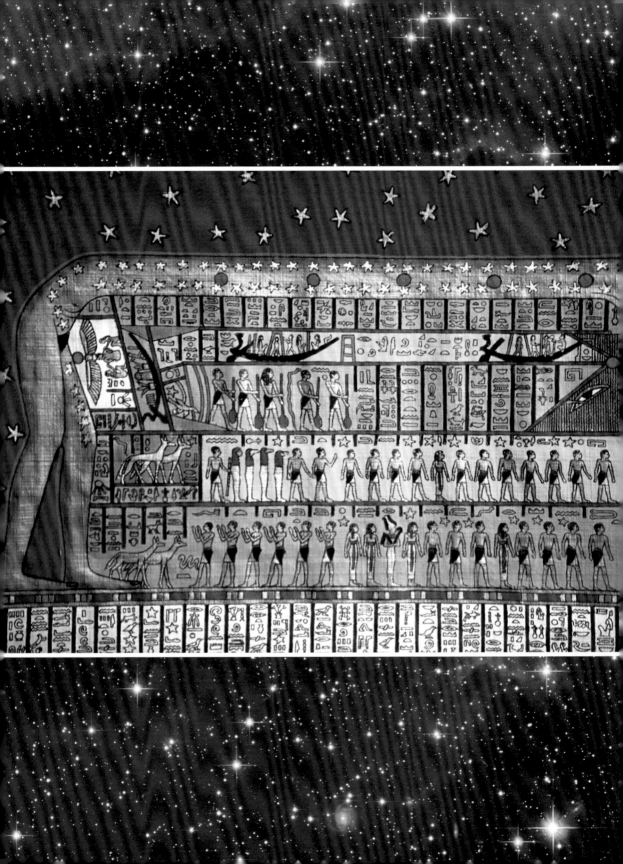

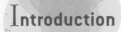

Introduction

For most of human history, people believed that the world was flat and that the sun and the moon circled it. People also believed that the sky was a solid dome not far overhead. They thought the stars were attached to this dome like lanterns.

Early humans held different beliefs about Earth and sky than modern humans do. But studying the heavens was just as important to them as it is to us. The regular movements of the sun, the moon, and the stars helped people measure the passing of time. These movements also marked important events in the year.

ANCIENT COSMOLOGIES

Life in ancient Egypt, which flourished from about 3150 to 30 B.C., revolved around the annual flooding of the Nile River. This flooding deposited rich soil on the farmland along the river. The Egyptians noticed that the bright star Sirius appeared in the sky just before the Nile flooded, so they created a calendar that began with this important event.

Celestial observations were also important to the ancient Egyptians' religion. They believed that Earth was a flat plain at the center of the universe. Over Earth arched the body of Nut, the goddess of the sky and mother of the sun, the moon, and the stars. Each day Ra, the sun god and creator of all living things, traveled through the sky and the underworld in a boat. Egyptian priests made calculations that described the motions of Nut, Ra, and other gods of the sky and Earth.

Every ancient culture had a different idea of what the universe was like. The Egyptians believed that Nut, the goddess of the sky, arched her body over Earth. The fertile lands of the Nile lay below her, the stars above.

CARTH CLOCK

Ancient humans used the changing positions of the sun, the moon, and the stars to mark the passage of time. Modern humans know that the changes we see in the sky result from Earth's movement through space.

The time Earth takes to rotate on its axis once is one day. Earth takes one year to circle once around the sun. Earth's axis is tipped 23.45°. This means that most of the time, part of Earth is tipped toward the sun and is getting more sunlight and warmth, while another part of Earth is tipped away and is getting less sunlight and warmth. When the Northern Hemisphere (the half of Earth north of the equator) is tilted toward the sun, the sun appears high in the sky and northern days are longer. The weather is warmer, and the Northern Hemisphere experiences summer. Six months later, the Northern Hemisphere is tilted away from the sun. The sun appears low in the sky, and northern days are shorter. The temperature grows cold, and the Northern Hemisphere experiences winter. Meanwhile, the opposite occurs in the Southern Hemisphere. When it's summer in the Northern Hemisphere, it's winter in the Southern Hemisphere.

During roughly the same period, the city-state of Babylon flourished in Mesopotamia (modern Iraq). Babylonian astronomers believed that the universe consisted of six levels: three heavens and three earths. Two heavens lay above the sky. The sky was the lowest heaven and contained the stars. Beneath the sky was the earth on which humans lived. Below this lay two underworlds.

Babylonians believed that the sun, the moon, and the stars directly affected human lives and that their motions predicted both fortune and calamity. For this reason, the Babylonians carefully recorded the positions of the stars and planets and the rising and setting of the sun and the moon. These observations are among humankind's oldest scientific records. The Babylonians used their observations to create horoscopes. Babylonian rulers and military leaders used their horoscopes as key decision-making aids.

ENTER THE BIBLE

Babylonian cosmology laid the foundation for the descriptions of the universe in the Judeo-Christian Bible. The Bible was written by multiple authors between about 1500 B.C. and A.D. 100. The authors of the Bible took great pains to describe Earth and its place in the universe. They said Earth is flat, square or rectangular in shape, with four corners. Giant pillars support it. Vast waters lie beneath Earth, and a domed sky covers it. Water lies above the

The Babylonians lived nearly three thousand years ago. They thought the Earth was a mountain surrounded by a vast sea beyond which were towering mountains no one could pass. The sky was a dome stretched over the world, and the stars were fastened to the inside of that dome.

dome. Sometimes windows in the dome open, and rain pours through. Earth lies motionless at the center of the universe. Everything else circles Earth. The Bible also explains how God created Earth specifically for humans as a unique place in the universe.

The Bible says Earth is flat and supported by huge pillars. The sky is a solid dome with doors and windows through which snow and rain fall. Earth doesn't move. Instead, the sun and the moon travel around it.

While the Bible took shape, Greek scientists started pondering the structure of the universe. Ancient Greek civilization flourished from about the 700s B.C. to the A.D. 500s. Earth's shape, position, and motion were not moral issues to the Greeks. So they were free to speculate about the nature of the universe. They proposed ideas that were more scientifically accurate, contrasting sharply with biblical cosmology.

Throughout early Christianity, biblical cosmology was an integral part of the faith. Religious leaders accepted only theories that agreed with the Bible. For centuries Christians generally accepted the church as the ultimate authority on everything. They considered it sinful to doubt the church. So if the church said Earth was at the center of the universe, then that was that. In addition, the church grew rich and powerful and those who voiced their doubts about church doctrine publicly faced punishment—even death.

Early Christian leaders discouraged curiosity about the natural world. They said studying Earth and the universe around it was a waste of time. Such study distracted people from studying God. Church leaders advised people to look inward for truth rather than ask questions about the exterior world. "Go not out of doors," said Saint Augustine (A.D. 354-430), a key figure in early Christianity. "Return into thyself. In the inner man dwells truth."

For nearly one thousand years, most Christians took Saint Augustine's words to heart. They abandoned science. Few asked questions about the world around them. No one dared to contradict the church.

But eventually a few people realized that biblical cosmology didn't quite match what they saw around them. They began to ask questions. This book is about those questions and the people who asked them.

Chapter 1

A World of Greek Ideas

The science of modern Western cosmology evolved out of the thinking of the ancient Greeks. The early Greeks had many different ideas about the structure of the universe. For example, the Greek epic poems *Iliad* and *Odyssey*, written during the 700s B.C., describe Earth as a huge, flat-topped mountain. This world-mountain is a circular island and surrounded by Oceanus, the world-ocean. The atmosphere just above Earth is thick with clouds and mist, but higher up it is clear. From the rim of Oceanus rises the dome of the sky. The sun, the moon, and the stars rise from the ocean at the edge of the sky-dome. After moving in an arc across the sky, they sink into the ocean on the opposite side of the dome. This description and similar ones were common among early European and Asian civilizations.

A Greek philosopher named Thales (624–546 B.C.) suggested that the universe is a hollow ball. The lower half of the ball is filled with water. Earth is a disk floating on the surface of the water. The sun, the moon, and the stars move freely in the clear, empty upper half of the ball.

Three thousand years ago, the ancient Greeks imagined a world that consisted of a flat disk-shaped continent surrounded by water.

A student of Thales named Anaximander (610–546 B.C.) suggested that Earth is a thick disk, like a hockey puck. On top of this disk is an ocean surrounded by a ring of mountains. In the center of this ocean is the known world in which humans live. Earth lies at rest at the center of the universe, surrounded by air. Around the air lie one or more hollow spheres with holes, beyond which lies a rim of fire. Humans see the fire shining through the holes as the sun, the moon, and the stars.

The Greek thinker Pythagoras (570–495 B.C.) pictured the universe as a vast hollow sphere. At the center of the sphere rests a great fire, the hearth of the universe. This is so far away from Earth that no one can see it. Revolving around this fire are ten concentric spheres. The outermost sphere contains the stars. The next five spheres hold the five planets known at the time. The next two spheres contain the sun and the moon. The two innermost spheres hold Earth and Counter-Earth. Counter-Earth is a twin planet that's opposite of Earth in every way.

NEW WAYS OF THINKING

New ideas about the universe were unpopular among the Greeks. For example, leaders of the Greek city of Athens banished scientist and philosopher Anaxagoras around 434 B.C. for suggesting that the sun is much smaller than previously thought. He said it was a white-hot stone about 35 miles (56 kilometers) wide and 4,000 miles (6,437 km) away.

Meanwhile, a handful of Greek philosophers started asking tricky questions about the universe. Eudoxus (410–347 B.C.), for example, believed that Earth lay at the center of the universe. But existing ideas about the structure of the universe did not explain some of the celestial motions Eudoxus observed.

Five stars caused a big problem for ancient astronomers. All the other stars in the sky moved together from east to west. Because they looked as though they were bright lights firmly attached to a moving dome, they were called the fixed stars. The five problem stars moved among the fixed stars like boats sailing among ships at anchor. The Greeks called these stars *planet*, or "the wanderers."

THE PROBLEM OF THE PLANETS

Eudoxus and Ptolemy tackled the phenomenon of retrograde motion. Retrograde motion is an apparent reversal of a planet's normal motion against the background of stars. Most of the time, a planet will appear to move from east to west. For a short time each year, a planet will appear to drift to a stop and then begin moving west to east. After a while, it stops again and then starts to move east to west again.

The planets aren't really moving in loops through the sky. Retrograde motion is an effect of perspective. As Earth and the other planets move around the sun, they catch up with and then overtake one another. This phenomenon is something like driving a car past another car moving along the same road. As you pass, the other car seems to move backward—even though it may be going almost as fast as you are.

To explain the motion of the planets, Eudoxus suggested that Earth lies motionless at the center of the universe. Several transparent, concentric spheres like glass bubbles envelop Earth. Each sphere can rotate in any direction. All the fixed stars are attached to the outermost sphere. The sphere rotates slowly, causing the stars' motion through the night sky. The next sphere carries the planet Saturn. Inside that are six more spheres carrying Jupiter, Mars, the sun, Venus, Mercury, and the moon, respectively.

Another Greek scientist named Aristotle (384–322 B.C.) was one of the first to consider the possibility that Earth is a sphere. He offered a variety of reasons to support this idea. For example, he noted that when Earth passes between the sun and the moon, Earth casts a shadow on the moon. (This event is called a lunar eclipse.) The shadow is round. Earth could cast a round shadow only if it is shaped like a ball. Aristotle also proposed that just as water in a falling drop forms a sphere, all the parts of Earth tend to move toward a center until they compact to form a sphere. Finally, he pointed out that southern constellations appear higher in the sky as one travels south. Only a spherical Earth could cause this effect.

Like many other early Greek scientists, Aristotle did not perform experiments to test his ideas. When it came to astronomy, Aristotle supported Eudoxus. He firmly believed that Earth lies motionless at the center of the universe. All the other heavenly bodies move around Earth in concentric spheres. "It is clear that the earth does not move, and that it does not lie elsewhere than at the center," Aristotle declared.

"It is clear that the earth does not move, and that it does not lie elsewhere than at the center."
—Aristotle, On the Heavens, *circa 350 B.C.*

Very few thinkers questioned this Earth-centered cosmology. The few who did faced ridicule. Alternate ideas, such as a universe in which Earth circles the sun, were difficult to test. They also seemed to defy observation and common sense.

The Greek scientist Aristarchus (310–230 B.C.) was the first known person to propose a sun-centered model of the universe. He suggested that Earth is one of many planets orbiting the sun. He said the apparent motion of the sun, the moon, the stars, and the planets around Earth is an illusion. The celestial bodies seem to move through the sky because Earth rotates on its axis. A contemporary of Aristarchus, the ancient Greek engineer Archimedes (287–212 B.C.), explained the theory:

> Aristarchus of Samos [proposes that] . . . the universe is many times greater than it is presently thought to be. His hypotheses are that the fixed stars and the sun remain motionless, that the

earth revolves about the sun in the circumference of a circle, the sun lying in the middle of the orbit, and that the sphere of the fixed stars, situated about the same center as the sun, is so great that the circular orbit of the earth is as small as a point compared with that sphere.

Aristarchus was correct. But his fellow scientists ignored and forgot his ideas.

THE MAN WHOSE WORD WAS LAW

Like most of his predecessors, Ptolemy (A.D. 90–168) favored an Earth-centered universe. He also believed that Earth was motionless. If Earth rotated, he explained, birds would have their perches snatched out from under their feet.

To explain the motions of the sun, the moon, the stars, and the planets, Ptolemy took Eudoxus's theory one step further. Ptolemy's idea was a complicated arrangement of overlapping circles. According to Ptolemy, each planet moved in a perfect circle around Earth. To explain the planets' wanderings, he proposed that as each planet moved along its orbit, it also moved in a smaller circle called an epicycle.

GEOCENTRIC VERSUS HELIOCENTRIC

A solar system in which the sun and the planets orbit Earth is geocentric. This word comes from the Greek words *geo*, which means "Earth," and *centric*, which means "center."

A solar system in which Earth and the other planets orbit the sun is heliocentric. This word comes from the Greek words *helio*, which means "sun," and *centric*.

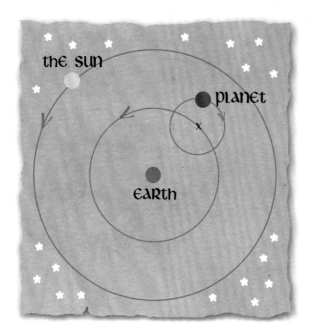

the sun

planet

x

EARTH

To explain the motions of the sun, the moon, and the planets, Ptolemy had to invent a complex system of orbits, cycles, and epicycles. This eventually became so complicated that some people began to wonder if there might be a simpler explanation.

To construct his theory, Ptolemy used the detailed measurements of star positions created by the great mathematician and astronomer Hipparchus (190–120 B.C.). Because Ptolemy used accurate data, his epicycles gave pretty accurate predictions about eclipses and planetary movements. And because Ptolemy's epicycles adequately explained the heavenly motions while preserving the idea of a central, unmoving Earth, the Christian Church embraced his theory enthusiastically.

With the church's support, the ideas of Aristotle and Ptolemy acquired almost as much authority as the Bible itself. Before long Ptolemy's theory became an official Christian doctrine, which held sway over the Christian world for nearly fifteen hundred years. Anyone expressing doubts about Ptolemy's cosmology risked imprisonment, torture, and death. Yet even with such threats facing them, a few brave souls dared to ask, "Could Ptolemy have been wrong?"

Chapter 2

The Copper Merchant's Son

The son of a copper merchant, Nicolaus Copernicus was born in 1473. He was raised by his mother's brother, Lucas Watzenrode, in Lidzbark, Poland. Watzenrode was a high-ranking church and government official of Warmia, a region of northern Poland. He saw to educating young Nicolaus so he could obtain a career in the church. Such a position would guarantee Copernicus a lifetime job that carried great respect and high social status.

Copernicus enrolled at the University of Krakow in 1491. He never earned a degree in religion—or anything else—at Krakow. But he did discover a love for mathematics and astronomy there. He began collecting books on the subjects and eventually amassed a huge personal library.

Copernicus continued his education from 1496 to 1503 at the University of Bologna in Italy, where he studied church law. There he met astronomy professor Domenico Maria Novara. While almost every other professor of astronomy in Europe taught Ptolemy's cosmology, Novara dared to question it. This planted a seed in Copernicus's mind that eventually grew into a great idea. Copernicus also studied medicine at Italy's University of Padova and in 1503 received a doctorate in church law from the University of Ferrara in Italy. For several years, he served as his uncle's personal secretary and doctor. After Watzenrode's death, Copernicus took a job at Frombork Cathedral in Poland. He lived and worked there for the rest of his life.

LITTLE COMMENTARY, BIG IDEA

If Copernicus thought that life in Frombork would allow him more time for astronomy, he was wrong. His church job was demanding, and he also served as a jurist (law specialist), translator, civil administrator, diplomat, and economist. His medical skills were in constant demand, and he even painted portraits of his friends.

Still, he spent every moment he could spare studying the night sky. In 1514 he set up an observatory in one of the cathedral's towers. In the 1500s, observatories included instruments to measure the positions of the sun, the moon, the planets, and the stars. These instruments did not include the telescope, however. It hadn't been invented yet. Frombork's location near the Baltic Sea wasn't ideal. The nights were often foggy, and Copernicus's poor eyesight didn't help either.

Around 1514 Copernicus wrote a short six-page essay called *Commentariolus* (Little Commentary). In it he introduced an idea

Copernicus made his groundbreaking astronomical observations from Frombork Cathedral in northern Poland *(facing page top)*. Copernicus was thought to have been buried at the cathedral, and in 2010, using modern DNA and other forensic technology, experts positively identified remains under the building's floor as Copernicus's.

THE ASTRONOMER'S TOOLS

Before the invention of the telescope in the early 1600s, astronomers had many tools for observing the universe. Most were for accurately measuring the positions and movements of the stars and the planets. Tools for determining what stars were made of or how far away they were had not yet been invented. In Copernicus's time, astronomers used instruments such as the astrolabe (*right*) and the quadrant to determine the positions of stars and to measure the distances between them. Star movements helped people anticipate the seasons, and they helped sailors guide their ships.

that may have grown from the seed of doubt about Ptolemy's cosmology sown by Professor Novara in Italy. Copernicus wrote that Ptolemy's epicycles "present no small difficulty." They did not match the universe Copernicus saw and didn't explain everything about planetary motion.

"Therefore," Copernicus decided, "having become aware of these [defects], I often considered whether there could perhaps be found a more reasonable arrangement of circles, from which every apparent irregularity would be derived while everything in itself would move uniformly, as is required by the rule of perfect motion." Copernicus believed a simpler explanation for celestial motions must exist.

In *Commentariolus* Copernicus proposed a new cosmology based on several assumptions:

1. Earth is the center of the moon's orbit.
2. All the planets orbit the sun, which is near the center of the universe.
3. The universe is much larger than previously thought.
4. Earth's distance to the sun is a small fraction of the size of the universe.
5. The apparent motion of the stars and the sun through the sky is a result of Earth's motion.
6. Retrograde motion is an illusion created by Earth's motion.

Copernicus didn't publish *Commentariolus*. Instead, he sent handwritten copies to a few close friends. He explained that the essay merely outlined his ideas—and for easier reading, he'd left out the mathematics. By distributing *Commentariolus*, Copernicus hoped to get feedback that would help him fully develop his theory. A handful of readers objected to Copernicus's heliocentric system because it contradicted the Bible. But most of his friends were excited about it. They encouraged Copernicus to continue his work.

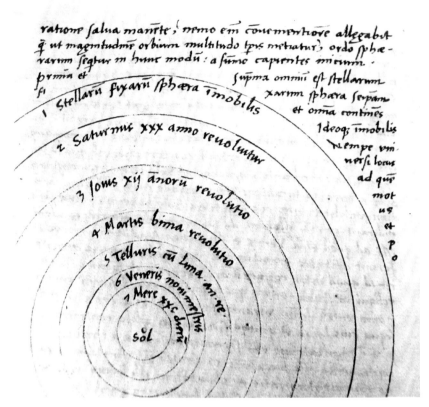

REVOLUTION

More than twenty years went by. In 1539 Georg Joachim Rheticus, a mathematician from Wittenberg, Germany, visited Copernicus to study with him. When Rheticus arrived, Copernicus had nearly finished a great six-volume work. The first volume contained a basic outline of his heliocentric theory. The other volumes contained mostly detailed proofs and related subjects. Copernicus called the complete work *De revolutionibus orbium coelesitim* (On the revolutions of the heavenly bodies), or *De revolutionibus* for short.

In Copernicus's work *De revolutionibus* (published in 1543), the Polish astronomer announced a revolutionary new vision of the universe. This drawing from the original manuscript shows the sun (Sol) at the center of the solar system.

Rheticus's visit was a stroke of good luck for Copernicus. Frombork was far from centers of scientific research and thinking. Copernicus had few people nearby who understood his interest in astronomy or who even cared about his new ideas. During the two years that Rheticus studied with Copernicus, Rheticus wrote a book, *Narratio prima* (First report). This book described the ideas behind Copernicus's heliocentric theory.

Rheticus and many of Copernicus's friends begged Copernicus to publish *De revolutionibus*. Encouraged by the friendly reception of *Commentariolus*, Copernicus agreed to do so. Rheticus oversaw the printing in 1543 in Germany, where he could be sure the book would be of the highest quality.

Copernicus suffered a severe stroke at this time. Legend has it that Rheticus handed him a copy of the finished *De revolutionibus* on his deathbed. The great astronomer was said to be holding it when he died on May 24, 1543.

CLOUDS ON THE HORIZON

Few people challenged Copernicus's heliocentric theory while he was alive. In fact, Nicholas Schönberg, Cardinal of Capua, Italy, wrote to Copernicus in 1536. In the letter, the high-powered church official said:

> Some years ago . . . I . . . learned that you had not merely mastered the discoveries of the ancient astronomers uncommonly well but had also formulated a new cosmology. In it you maintain that the earth moves; that the sun occupies the lowest, and thus the central, place in the universe. . . . Therefore with the utmost earnestness I entreat you . . . to communicate this discovery of yours to scholars.

In Copernicus's Words

De revolutionibus contained two especially revolutionary ideas. The first idea concerned the relationship of the planets to the sun:

> Venus and Mercury revolve around the sun and cannot go farther away from it than the circles of their orbits permit. . . . According to this theory, then, Mercury's orbit should be included inside the orbit of Venus. . . . If, acting upon this supposition, we connect Saturn, Jupiter, and Mars with the same center, keeping in mind the greater extent of their orbits . . . we cannot fail to see the explanation of the regular order of their motions. This proves sufficiently that their center belongs to the sun.

The second idea concerned the place of the solar system in the universe:

> The extent of the universe . . . is so great that, whereas the distance of the earth from the sun is considerable in comparison with the other planetary orbits, it disappears when compared to the sphere of the fixed stars. I hold this to be more easily comprehensible than when the mind is confused by [Ptolemy's] almost endless number of circles, which is necessarily the case with those who keep the earth in the middle of the universe.

But by the time *De revolutionibus* was published, some people were getting cold feet about the idea of a sun-centered universe. The nervous publisher slipped a foreword in the book without the knowledge of Rheticus or Copernicus. In it Andreas Osiander, a well-known German theologian, defended *De revolutionibus*:

> There have already been widespread reports about the novel hypotheses of this work, which declares that the earth moves whereas the sun is at rest in the center of the universe. . . . [T]hese hypotheses need not be true nor even probable. On the contrary, if they provide a calculus consistent with the observations, that alone is enough. . . . So far as hypotheses are concerned, let no one expect anything certain from astronomy, which cannot furnish it, lest he accept as the truth ideas conceived for another purpose, and depart from this study a greater fool than when he entered it.

So, Osiander was saying that Copernicus's theory was just a mathematical curiosity. It had nothing to do with reality.

A REVOLUTION IN SCIENCE

In the decades preceding and following the publication of *De revolutionibus*, a cultural movement known as the Renaissance affected all European arts and sciences. Explorers sailed around the world, confirming at last that Earth is a sphere. They also learned that Earth is much bigger than anyone had previously thought. They discovered entirely unknown continents. Great advances occurred in mathematics, including the invention of the first calculating machines, telescopes, and microscopes. Scientists performed the first experiments with magnetism and electricity.

Renaissance thinkers realized that an idea wasn't necessarily true just because it had been taught for centuries. The new scientists performed experiments, using mathematics to test old theories such as Aristotle and Ptolemy's geocentric universe.

Copernicus was one of these daring new scientists. He found that an Earth-centered solar system crumbled under mathematical scrutiny. Ptolemy had assumed that Earth must be in the center of the solar system. Then he justified this belief with mathematics. As he observed facts that didn't support his key assumption, he made his theory more and more complicated to keep Earth in the center. Eventually Ptolemy's solar system became ridiculously complex.

Copernicus, on the other hand, developed his theory *from* mathematics. He didn't care what the math might show. If Earth turned up elsewhere than the center of the solar system, so be it. This was a very different approach to astronomy than his predecessors had used.

GATHERING STORM

Religious objections to Copernicus's cosmology were slow in coming. The Catholic Church had few problems with the theory at first. Most Catholic leaders agreed with Osiander: Copernicus's idea was merely a way to simplify astronomical calculations. They said Copernicus wasn't suggesting that Earth really orbited the sun. Copernicus was a loyal Catholic and a respected church official. He had carefully gained the church's permission before publishing *De revolutionibus*. He had even dedicated it to Pope Paul III. Many Catholic universities included it in their astronomy and mathematics courses. Copernicus's calculations of planetary movements even formed the basis for the new calendar established by Pope Gregory XIII in the late 1500s.

Protestant officials, however, weren't so accepting. In 1539 Protestant leader Martin Luther objected to Copernicus's heliocentric theory:

> There is talk of a new [astronomer] who wants to prove that the earth moves and goes around instead of the sky, the sun, the moon, just as if somebody were moving in a carriage or ship might hold that he was sitting still and at rest while the earth and the trees walked and moved. But that is how things are nowadays: when a man wishes to be clever he must needs invent something special, and the way he does it must needs be the best! The fool wants to turn the whole art of astronomy upside down.

Copernicus's idea of a moving Earth contradicted the Bible. Luther believed the Bible was the ultimate authority, so he felt Copernicus must be wrong. Many other Protestant leaders echoed Luther's objections. They pointed to Bible passages that refuted Copernicus's theory. For example, Psalm 93 says, "Indeed, the world is firmly established, it will not be moved." And Psalm 104 declares, "He established the earth upon its foundations, so that it will not totter forever and ever."

Heliocentrism caused serious problems for Bible believers. Demoting Earth from its central position implied a demotion of humankind from the center of God's attention. And it made people wonder, "If the universe is really infinite, where can God and heaven be, and how can humankind possibly find them?" These questions were especially troubling for Protestants, who interpreted the Bible more literally than Catholics did. Many Protestant leaders began calling Copernicus and his supporters heretics. They wanted to ban *De revolutionibus* and forbid Christians to read or discuss it. But in the 1500s, Protestants did not yet have the power and reach of the Catholic Church. Though Protestant leaders deplored Copernicus's theory, they couldn't do much about it.

Chapter 3

The Reluctant Astrologer

Johannes Kepler was born in Weil der Stadt, Germany, in 1571. He was a sickly child, but he had a brilliant mind with a remarkable talent for mathematics. With his number skills, he often amazed visitors at the inn where his mother worked. Kepler's mother encouraged an interest in astronomy and astrology. In 1577, when Kepler was six years old, a large comet appeared in the sky. His mother took him to a nearby hill to look at it. Three years later, she woke him in the middle of the night so he could see a lunar eclipse.

In 1589 Kepler enrolled at Germany's University of Tübingen. A devout Lutheran who wanted to become a minister, he studied theology—but he excelled in mathematics. When he learned of Copernicus's theory, he quickly accepted it. Its simplicity appealed to his logical mind.

In 1594 Kepler accepted a job teaching science and mathematics at a Protestant school in the city of Graz, Austria. He was glad to leave Tübingen. He had been miserable there. Aloof, argumentative, and gloomy, he had made no friends. He had become withdrawn and lonely. But his new job suited him. It allowed him the freedom to think about the universe and work on the mathematics he believed ran it.

The appearance of the Great Comet of 1577 frightened people all over Europe. However, it inspired the young Johannes Kepler to a lifelong passion for astronomy and mathematics.

In 1596 Kepler published his first book, *Mysterium cosmographicum* (Cosmographic mystery). It contained page after page of dense mysticism about the role of three-dimensional geometrical solids in the structure of the universe. Although *Mysterium* was not widely read, it was the first book to defend Copernicus's heliocentric theory. It also established Kepler's reputation as a gifted mathematician.

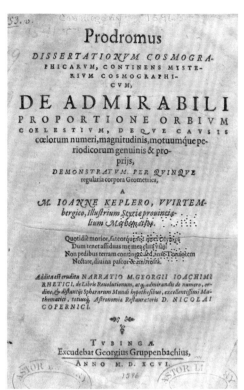

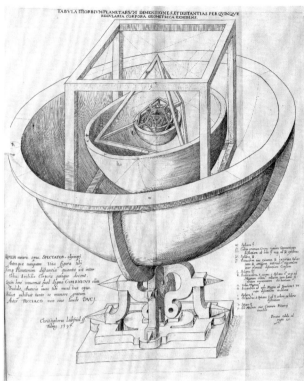

The title page *(above left)* and an illustration from Kepler's first book, the *Mysterium cosmographicum* (1596). Kepler was a strange mixture of mysticism and science. The diagram *(right)* illustrates his belief in a connection between the orbits of the planets and the regular polygons.

To continue developing the ideas in *Mysterium*, Kepler needed the best observations of the stars and the planets ever made. But he had an eye condition called polyopia, which caused him to see multiple images. He needed some help.

The best astronomical observations and measurements in the world at that time came from Tycho Brahe, a Danish nobleman and astronomer living and working in Prague, Bohemia (modern Czech Republic). Tycho was impressed with the mathematical genius behind *Mysterium*, and in 1599, he invited Kepler to join his team. Kepler accepted and moved to Prague the next year.

TYCHO BRAHE

Tycho Brahe was born to a wealthy noble Danish family in 1546 and was raised by his uncle Jorgen. Tycho enrolled at the University of Copenhagen in 1559 to prepare for a political career. A solar eclipse the next year turned his attention toward astronomy. Fascinated, he promptly read a copy of Ptolemy's work. In 1563, at the age of seventeen, he began recalculating the movements of the planets. He had found many discrepancies between predicted and observed positions. He decided that his life's work would be to make astronomy more accurate.

Tycho's work gained fame all over Europe. King Frederik II of Denmark offered him an island and the funds to build an observatory there. Tycho's observatory opened in 1576. He named it Uraniborg (Castle of Urania). Urania is the Greek muse, or inspiration, of astronomers.

Tycho totally rejected Copernicus's theory and instead constructed his own theory. It combined the worst aspects of Ptolemy's cosmology with some original—and confusing—ideas Tycho stole from Paul Wittich, a German astronomer who'd visited Uraniborg. Tycho was a poor theorist, but he was a brilliant observer. At Uraniborg he made the most accurate celestial measurements anyone had ever created. Uraniborg became the astronomical capital of Europe. Tycho lost Uraniborg when King Frederik died in 1588. Tycho eventually settled in Prague, where he found support from the king of Bohemia, Rudolf II. He built a new observatory and hired an assistant, a young German mathematician named Johannes Kepler.

Kepler and Tycho were polar opposites. Kepler was a serious, often depressed loner. Tycho was a flamboyant, lively, popular man. He was rich and always seemed to be hosting a party in his fabulous home. "Tycho," said Kepler, "is superlatively rich but knows not how to make use of it. Any single instrument of his costs more than my and my whole family's fortunes put together."

KEPLER AND TYCHO

Kepler hoped that Tycho's data would help him prove a geometrical theory about the planets' orbits. But Tycho was very secretive and would release only small snippets of data. "Tycho," Kepler complained, "gave me no opportunity to share in his experiences. He would only . . . mention, as if in passing, today the figure of the apogee of one planet, tomorrow the nodes of another." (Apogee and node refer to points along the orbit of a celestial body.)

Meanwhile, Kepler wondered what kept the moon orbiting Earth and the planets orbiting the sun. He thought a force such as magnetism might connect the celestial bodies. "There is a force in the earth which causes the moon to move," he wrote. He was right. But the world wouldn't identify that force until Isaac Newton came along decades later.

Tycho died suddenly on October 24, 1601. Two days later, Kepler succeeded Tycho as official mathematician to Rudolf II, the king of Bohemia. Though Kepler had worked with Tycho for only one year, no one else was better suited to the job. Kepler's new position consisted mostly of creating horoscopes for the king and other nobles. He did this very well. Kepler did not really approve of astrology, but Rudolf was paying him well to do it. And even better, Kepler's new job gave him full use of all Tycho's data and the freedom and time to analyze it to his heart's content.

Using Copernicus's theory and Tycho's data on the motion of Mars, Kepler set out to calculate Mars's complete orbit. It took him more than two years and five hundred pages of calculations to discover that Copernicus's theory didn't precisely match the observed movement of Mars. The difference was extremely small, but Kepler was positive that he had made no mathematical mistakes. He was also sure that Tycho's measurements were correct. And he was convinced that Copernicus's theory was correct too.

The discrepancy had to have a cause. But what could it possibly be? He said about his urge to discover the answer:

> The testimony of the ages confirms that the motions of the planets are orbicular. It is an immediate presumption of reason, reflected in experience, that their gyrations are perfect circles. For among figures it is circles, and among the bodies the heavens, that are considered the most perfect. However when experience is seen to teach something deviate from a simple circular path, it gives rise to a powerful sense of wonder, which at length drives men to look into causes.

MAKE YOUR OWN ELLIPSE

An ellipse is a flattened circle. A circle has a single center point, but an ellipse has two center points. Each of these is called a focus, and together they are called foci. The farther apart the foci are, the flatter the ellipse is. The closer together the foci are, the rounder the ellipse is. An ellipse with both foci in the same spot is a circle.

It's easy to draw an ellipse. Take a length of string and tie the ends together to make a closed loop. Place the loop around a pair of thumbtacks or pushpins stuck into a piece of cardboard. Make sure the loop fits loosely around the tacks. Put the point of a pencil inside the loop. Pull the string taut, and keep it taut while tracing a pencil line all the way around the tacks. The shape you trace is an ellipse. The tacks mark the foci of the ellipse. You can make different ellipses by moving the tacks closer together or farther apart.

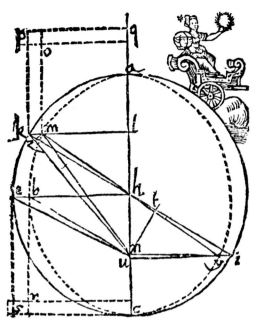

A COURAGEOUS DECISION

No matter how he manipulated the math, Kepler couldn't make Tycho's observations on the movement of Mars match the circular orbits described by Copernicus. Finally, Kepler plotted Tycho's observed positions of Mars on paper. Kepler had been expecting to see a perfect circle, but he saw a different figure instead—an ellipse.

In this drawing from Kepler's book *Astronomia nova* (1609), he illustrates his discovery that the orbit of Mars is an ellipse (dotted line) and not a circle (solid line).

The difference between Mars's elliptical orbit and a circular orbit was very small. But it was enough to account for the difference between Tycho's data and Copernicus's theory. For several reasons, Kepler hesitated to abandon the idea that the solar system operated in perfect circles. Kepler was a devoutly religious man. He believed a solar system based on perfect circles reflected God's own perfection. Important ancient Greek scientists as well as modern European theorists had assumed that the planets move in circles. Copernicus had said that "the mind shudders" at the thought of noncircular movement in the heavens, because it suggests an imperfect creation.

When facts contradict a cherished theory—especially a theory connected with religion—many people feel tempted to ignore the facts. But Kepler couldn't argue with the facts. He accepted that planetary orbits are elliptical. This took considerable courage.

KEPLER'S LAWS OF PLANETARY MOTION

Kepler's analysis of Mars's orbit resulted in a book titled *Astronomia nova* (New astronomy). This book, published in 1609, contains the first two of three laws that bear Kepler's name. Kepler's first law of planetary motion states that each planet in our solar system orbits the sun in an ellipse. The sun occupies one of the two focus points of the ellipse. The other focus is empty.

Kepler had noticed something else about the planets' orbits. Those closer to the sun moved faster than those farther away from the sun. Kepler's second law uses the concept of a planet's radius vector to explain why this is so.

A line from the center of the sun to the center of a planet is called the planet's radius vector. You can imagine the radius vector as the hand of a giant clock. As the hand moves from twelve to two o'clock, it sweeps across a wedge-shaped area. As the hand moves from two to six o'clock, it sweeps across a wedge-shaped area twice as large. In a circle—as in a clockface—it takes twice as long for the radius vector to sweep across an area twice as large. Or in an equal amount of time, the radius vector sweeps across an equal area.

Kepler discovered that something different happens as a planet moves along its elliptical orbit. As the planet orbits the sun, its radius vector sweeps across the area between the planet and the sun. Just like a clock hand, the planet's radius vector sweeps across equal areas in equal amounts of time. But to do this in an elliptical orbit, the planet must cover more distance along the ellipse when it's closer to the sun. So the planet has to travel faster.

Ten years later, in 1619, Kepler published a third law in his book *Harmonices mundi* (Harmony of the world). This law explains the relationship between a planet's orbital period (the length of time a planet takes to orbit the sun) and the planet's average distance from the sun. Kepler's third law of planetary motion states that a planet's orbital period increases dramatically with its distance from the sun.

THE FINAL YEARS

In 1620 Kepler's seventy-four-year-old mother was arrested for witchcraft. He went to Germany and found her chained in a dungeon in Leonberg, facing threats of torture and death. Kepler defended his mother at her trial by using science. He showed her accusers natural explanations for everything she had done, including how she had healed some of Leonberg's outstanding citizens. She simply practiced good medicine, he argued, not black magic. Thanks to Kepler, his mother was not burned at the stake like other accused witches. Instead, in 1621 Leonberg officials banished her for life.

In Kepler's last large-scale astronomical work, he created new tables of planetary motions based on his laws and Tycho's observations. Kepler completed the tables in 1623 and named them *Tabulae Rudolphinae* (Rudolphine Tables) after his late benefactor. Published in 1627, the tables provided the most accurate planetary data available at that time and remained so for nearly one hundred years.

"I measured the heavens,

Now the earth's shadows I measure

My mind was already in the heavens,

Now the shadow of my body rests."

—Johannes Kepler's self-written epitaph, 1630

The frontispiece of Kepler's final book, the Rudolphine Tables (1627), is filled with astrological symbols, images of famous astrologers and scientific instruments, and a map of the island of Hven, where Tycho had his observatory.

The world continued to feel Kepler's influence even after his death in 1630. He had predicted that Mercury would pass across the sun on November 7, 1631. That day astronomers across Europe watched a tiny black dot creep across the face of the sun, assuring Kepler's reputation as the greatest mathematician astronomy had ever known.

Chapter 4

Astronomy on Trial

Galileo Galilei was born in Pisa, Italy, on February 15, 1564. His family had ties to nobility, but they were not very rich. In 1581, when Galileo was seventeen, he enrolled at the University of Pisa. His father hoped he would study medicine. Instead, Galileo chose to study mathematics. Eight years later, the university appointed him chair of the mathematics department. In 1592 he moved to the University of Padova. He taught geometry, mechanics, and astronomy there for the next eighteen years.

Most Europeans in Galileo's time accepted Aristotle's earlier ideas about the universe without question. Galileo, however, had doubts. For instance, Aristotle had written that heavier objects fall faster than lighter objects. It seemed to make so much sense that no one thought to test it with an experiment. But Galileo did.

Galileo had started wondering about how things fall while working on pendulums. A pendulum is a weight hanging on the end of a cord. The other end of the cord is attached to a fixed point so the weight can swing freely. Galileo noticed that the size of the weight does not affect a pendulum's period. (The period is the time a pendulum takes to complete one cycle—a swing away from and back to its starting position.) A pendulum 6 feet (2 meters) long would swing as rapidly with a 1-pound (0.5-kilogram) weight as it would with a 10-pound (5 kg) weight. The length of the cord, however, does affect a pendulum's period. A pendulum with a short cord swings faster than a pendulum with a long cord.

Legend tells us that it was while Galileo was watching the pendulum at the Cathedral of Pisa swinging at the end of its long chain *(facing page top)* that he got his idea about how different weights fall.

Galileo mulled over these discoveries. He had observed that two pendulums of equal length swinging side by side will swing at the same rate, even if their weights are different. He wondered, If someone cuts the cords so the weights fall freely, won't they fall at the same speed?

To test his idea, Galileo rolled two balls—a smaller, lighter one and a larger, heavier one—down a ramp. The balls reached the end of the ramp at exactly the same time. Galileo also dropped different weights from different heights. They all fell at the same speed. He wrote about his discoveries in a book called *De motu* (On motion). At the time, Galileo did not suspect that his work had anything to do with astronomy. It took almost one hundred years before anyone discovered what the connection was.

AN EYE ON THE HEAVENS

In 1604 an exciting celestial event boosted Galileo's interest in astronomy. A supernova (an especially bright exploding star)

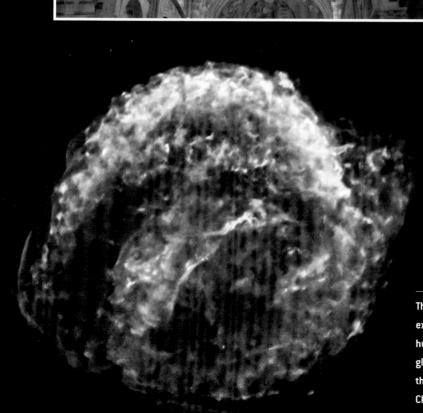

The star that Kepler saw explode in 1604 is now a huge, expanding cloud of glowing gas, as seen in this image taken by the Chandra X-ray Observatory, a telescope in outer space.

appeared in the sky. Many supernovas occur in our galaxy, but people can rarely see them with the naked eye. In Galileo's time, a supernova was unheard of—and frightening. Aristotle and other ancient philosophers had taught that the heavens were unchanging. Some scientists said that the new light in the sky could not possibly be a star, since Aristotle couldn't be wrong. They said it had to be a phenomenon in the upper atmosphere, such as a meteor (a chunk of stone or metal entering Earth's atmosphere).

Galileo had no special loyalty to Aristotle and insisted that the new light was a star. He proved that it was very far away from Earth by showing that no astronomer could detect its parallax (a change in the apparent position of a nearby object against the backdrop of farther objects). This proof did not gain many friends for Galileo.

PARALLAX

Parallax is a change in the apparent position of a nearby object against the backdrop of farther objects. In astronomy, parallax is the change in apparent position of a nearer celestial body against the backdrop of fixed stars when one measures the position from widely separated points. Measuring the position at different times of the year allows an observer to use distant points along Earth's orbit. The closer the object, the larger its parallax. When viewed from two different places, a nearer celestial body appears to move against the background stars. A very distant celestial body has no parallax because it is at least as far away as the fixed stars.

You can simulate parallax by holding up a finger at arm's length and closing one eye. Note where your finger lies against a backdrop of farther objects. Open your eye and close the other one. Notice how your finger seems to jump. This change in your finger's apparent position is parallax.

Galileo's telescope was a hollow tube a little more than 3 feet (0.9 m) long. It was made of wood and had a glass lens in either end. It could make distant objects appear twenty-one times larger.

By saying that a new star had just appeared, Galileo was suggesting—dangerously—that Aristotle and the church were wrong.

Galileo's interest in astronomy was radically impacted by a new and exciting instrument—the telescope. He wrote, "A report reached my ears that a Dutchman had constructed a telescope, by the aid of which visible objects, although at a great distance from the eye of the observer, were seen distinctly as if near." Galileo was an expert in optics (the study of the behavior and properties of light), so he quickly figured out how to make his own telescope. He made two lenses and then attached them to either end of a small lead tube. Galileo's telescope made distant objects seem three times closer. This was better than any Dutch telescope. Galileo then built another telescope. This one made objects seem six times nearer. Finally, he built a telescope that magnified distant objects by thirty times.

Magic Glasses

In 1608 the son of Hans Lippershey, an optician in Middleburg, Netherlands, made a discovery. The boy was playing with some lenses in his father's shop. He put one in front of the other and looked through them at the distant cathedral clock tower. To his surprise, the clock looked much nearer than it was. He told his father about his discovery. Lippershey came up with the idea of placing two lenses at either end of a tube and selling such devices as "magic glasses."

Legend says that Ambrogio Spinola, an Italian nobleman in the area at the time, was so pleased with Lippershey's toy that he showed it to Prince Maurice of Nassau, a Dutch general and statesman. Prince Maurice thought the telescope might prove useful during wartime. It would help him see approaching ships long before they were visible to the naked eye.

Lippershey realized that he might have invented something of great value. He applied to the Dutch government for a patent. The government turned him down. Officials saw no advantage to it, because a person could look through with only one eye at a time. With no patent protection, people could easily reproduce the telescope and it spread quickly across Europe.

Galileo took his improved telescope to Venice, Italy, and showed it to the officials there. "Many noblemen and senators," he wrote, "though of advanced age, mounted to the top of one of the highest towers to watch the ships which were visible through my glass two hours before they were seen entering the harbor, for it makes a thing fifty miles [80 km] off as near and clear as if it were only five [8 km]." So many government officials and noblemen wanted to look through Galileo's telescope that he complained its popularity was distracting him from his work.

Hardly anyone had thought of turning a telescope toward the

sky. The stars were nothing more than bright pinpoints of light. And everyone knew that the moon was a gleaming sphere of absolute purity. Its dark markings were only a reflection of the impure Earth. What could humans possibly gain from looking at the stars and the moon more closely?

STARRY MESSENGER

In 1609 and 1610, Galileo began making celestial observations with his telescope. The ancient Greek engineer Archimedes had said, "Give me a lever long enough and a fulcrum on which to place it, and I shall move the world." With a lever the size of a telescope, Galileo pried Earth from its place at the center of the universe.

What Galileo learned forever changed how we look at Earth and the heavens. He saw that the moon is covered with mountains and craters. It is, he said, "not smooth, uniform, and precisely spherical as a great number of philosophers believe it (and the other heavenly bodies) to be, but is uneven, rough, and full of cavities and prominences, being not unlike the face of the earth." As Galileo watched the shadows change on the moon's surface, he realized that the moon's light was actually reflected sunlight.

Planets and stars, he found, are completely different from each other. In the telescope, stars looked like points of light, "just as when they [are] viewed by simply looking at them," Galileo said. The planets, however, "present their discs perfectly round . . . and appear as so many little moons, completely illuminated and of a globular shape." Galileo saw that Venus, like the moon, goes through phases. Some of the planets have vague markings that Galileo thought might be continents and seas. He noted that even the sun, the most perfect of all the heavenly bodies, has spots.

When Galileo turned his telescope toward Jupiter, he made more surprising discoveries. "There were three little stars," Galileo wrote on January 7, 1610, "small but very bright, near the planet." At first he thought the objects were stars. But when he looked at Jupiter again on the following night, the three little stars had moved! He realized that Jupiter's "stars" are actually moons. These moons move "about Jupiter, as Venus and Mercury round the Sun," he wrote. Galileo had discovered not only that Jupiter is a world but also that it has moons. Earth was no longer the only world with a satellite (a celestial body orbiting another celestial body).

Galileo's observations led him to conclude that "Venus and Mercury revolve round the Sun, as do all the

Two pages from Galileo's book *Sidereus nuncius* (1610). The drawings show craters and mountains on the surface of the moon. Galileo was the first person in history to see these. They helped prove that the moon was a world not so unlike our own.

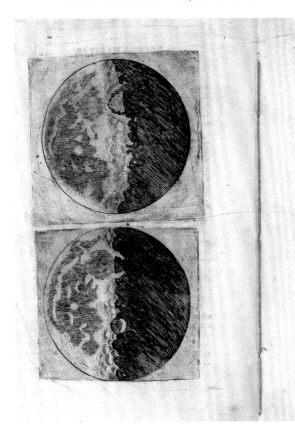

rest of the planets. A truth believed indeed by the Pythagorean school, by Copernicus, and by Kepler, but never proved by the evidence of our senses, as it is now proved in the case of Venus and Mercury." In 1610 Galileo published these discoveries and ideas in a book called *Sidereus nuncius* (Starry messenger). It was an immediate sensation. Because Galileo wrote in Italian instead of in Latin like other scholars and clergy, he developed a huge popular following. Three years later, Galileo published a book titled *Istoria e dimostrazioni intorno alle macchie solari e loro accidenti* (History and demonstrations concerning sunspots and their properties). In this book, he firmly supports Copernicus's cosmology.

ENEMY OF THE CHURCH

After the publication of his books, Galileo invited representatives from the Catholic Church to look through his telescope at the heavens. Most of them flatly refused. They said Jupiter's moons were simply an illusion. One clergyman asked why God wouldn't make it possible for us to see such things with the naked eye. Another said there was no point in looking for Jupiter's moons because the Bible didn't mention them, and therefore they didn't exist. The moon does not shine by reflected sunlight, said the clergymen, because the Bible clearly states that the moon is a "great light." And finally, a scholar argued that if the telescope were worth anything at all, the Greeks would have already invented it.

"PHILOSOPHY is written in this grand book, the universe. . . . It is written in the language of mathematics, and its characters are triangles, circles, and other geometric figures."
—*Galileo Galilei, 1623*

Before Galileo studied the heavens with his telescope, most

Christian leaders had supported Copernicus's theory. Galileo's discoveries changed the game. He found physical proof that Copernicus was right and Aristotle and Ptolemy were wrong. By doing so, Galileo was challenging the authority of the church, thereby making himself its enemy.

To show its strength in the face of Galileo's discoveries, the church suddenly forbade professors from teaching Copernican cosmology in universities. It also prohibited mention of Galileo's discoveries. From 1613 to 1633, Galileo was in constant communication with Catholic authorities in Rome. He desperately tried to defend his discoveries. But in 1616, the pope directed Cardinal Roberto Bellarmino to read an order to Galileo that he must neither hold nor defend Copernicus's theory. In 1624 Pope Urban VIII assured Galileo that he was free to discuss the theory as a mathematical tool. But if he so much as suggested that Copernicus's theory described the real universe, Galileo would be arrested.

"To Affirm that the Sun is really fixed in the center of the heavens and that the Earth revolves very swiftly around the Sun is a dangerous thing, not only irritating the theologians and philosophers, but injuring our holy faith and making the sacred scripture false."

—Roberto Bellarmino, early 1600s

Galileo was a hard man to stop, however. He knew he was right. He published a book, *Dialogo sopra i due massimi sistemi del mondo* (Dialogue concerning the two chief world systems), in 1632. It was a fictional debate between characters arguing for Ptolemy and Aristotle on one side and for Copernicus on the other. The defenders of Copernicus won the argument.

The frontispiece to Galileo's *Dialogo* (1632) shows two characters from the book trying to convince a third of the merits of the Copernican versus Ptolemaic systems. Since Galileo favored the former, he made that character sound much smarter than the one who argued for the old views.

AN IDEA ON TRIAL

The church was not amused. In 1633 church authorities ordered Galileo to stand trial before the dreaded Inquisition, a church court whose job was to identify and punish heretics. The church accused Galileo of ignoring Bellarmino's order. Galileo was clearly guilty. But the church was uncertain what to do with him. Galileo had become an internationally famous scientist, inventor, and scholar. If the church were to execute Galileo, as it had recently burned scientist Giordano Bruno at the stake for accepting Copernicus's heliocentric view of the universe, it would have to deal with protests all across Europe. Meanwhile, Galileo remained obstinate. He wrote to a friend and asked, "Why is it that we insist that whenever it speaks of the Sun or of the Earth, Holy Scripture be considered quite infallible?"

During the trial, church officials showed Galileo the instruments with which they planned to torture him if he failed to reject the Copernican system. Galileo was nearly seventy years old. He was going blind, and his health was deteriorating. He gave in and signed a prepared document in which he rejected his work. He knew this was an empty gesture. His book *Dialogo* was already available to thinking men and women all over the world. Galileo knew that no matter how hard the church tried, it couldn't stop the spread of knowledge about the solar system.

The church imprisoned Galileo instead of executing him. For five years, he lived under house arrest at his home in Arcetri, Italy. In 1638 the pope allowed the aging, blind scientist to move to his home in Florence, Italy, where he could be closer to his doctors. He died there in 1642. More than three hundred years later, the church issued a formal apology for mistakes such as the trials of the Inquisition. However, the church did not say it had been wrong to silence Galileo.

THE CHURCH CONDEMNS GALILEO

"We say, pronounce, sentence, and declare that you, the said Galileo, by reason of the matters adduced [cited] in trial, and by you confessed as above, have rendered yourself in the judgment of this Holy Office [the court of the Inquisition] vehemently suspected of heresy [denying church doctrine], namely, of having believed and held the doctrine—which is false and contrary to the sacred and divine Scriptures—that the Sun is the center of the world and does not move from east to west and that the Earth moves and is not the center of the world; and that an opinion may be held and defended as probable after it has been declared and defined to be contrary to the Holy Scripture; and that consequently you have incurred all the censures and penalties imposed and promulgated in the sacred canons [laws] and other constitutions, general and particular, against such delinquents [heretics]."

—Inquisition judges, 1633

In this nineteenth-century painting, artist Joseph-Nicolas Robert-Fleury shows Galileo *(front, second from left with white beard)* on trial before the judges of the Holy Office. His sentence for disobeying the church was to imprison him in his home for the rest of his life.

Chapter 5

The Lonely Giant

Isaac Newton was born in the village of Woolsthorpe, England, on Christmas Day in 1642, the same year Galileo died. He had a lonely and difficult childhood, retreating into the world of nature, science, and mechanics. In 1661, when he was nineteen, Newton went off to college at Cambridge University. Despite all the discoveries of the preceding two centuries, Cambridge still taught the astronomy of Aristotle and Ptolemy. Newton had little interest in the old science and was much more interested in the work of Copernicus, Kepler, and Galileo.

While wandering through a Cambridge street fair in 1663, Newton found a book about astrology. He read the book until he reached a page he didn't understand. This page required

THE ALCHEMIST

Newton was a strange product of ancient beliefs and modern science. He accepted every date and event in Greek and Roman mythology and in the Bible. A devoutly religious man, he did not doubt that God had created Earth around 4000 B.C., as Bible scholars had calculated, or that Adam and Eve had really existed. Newton spent months computing the size of Noah's ark. According to Newton, the biblical ark weighed exactly 18,231 tons (16,539 metric tons).

Newton was also obsessed with alchemy, an ancient philosophic and experimental practice related to the effort to change common substances into pure elements. In Newton's day, alchemy included everything from manufacturing paint pigments and medicines to making fake precious stones. It also included trying to make the so-called philosopher's stone. This, alchemists believed, was a magical substance that would cure other substances of their impurities. It could turn lead into gold and cure humans of their illnesses.

Newton practiced alchemy all his life. He often worked day and night conducting alchemical experiments in his laboratory. Historians who have studied Newton's alchemical notebooks believe he wanted to gain understanding of and power over nature rather than to gain wealth from his discoveries.

knowledge of trigonometry so he went to the bookstore and bought a book about trigonometry. He read it and discovered that it required knowledge of geometry. Back to the bookstore he went. This time he bought a copy of *Elements*, a book by the ancient Greek mathematician Euclid that describes the basic principles of geometry. Newton's interest in mathematics was born.

Newton earned his bachelor's degree in August 1665. Shortly thereafter, Cambridge University closed temporarily. The closure was a precaution against the deadly bubonic plague sweeping through London, only 50 miles (80 km) away. Newton fled to Woolsthorpe, where he remained for eighteen months. In his lonely retreat, he came up with many ideas that he would spend the rest of his scientific career refining. For example, he began developing calculus, an entirely new branch of mathematics. While he was at it, he also made key discoveries about light and gravitation. "In those days," he wrote, "I was in the prime of my age for invention and minded mathematics and [science] more than at any time since."

THE ABSENTMINDED PROFESSOR

Newton returned to Cambridge University when it reopened in 1667. He earned a master's degree the next year and became a professor of mathematics in 1670. In 1671 he was elected a Fellow of the Royal Society, the highest honor a British scientist can receive.

Newton was totally devoted to his research. He never took a break, never went riding or walking, and never played games. He often showed up to deliver lectures with his long, gray hair uncombed, his shoes untied, and his clothes wrinkled and tattered. He was as unskilled at ordinary life as he was brilliant in science. For example, legend says he cut a hole in the door of his house so his cat could come and go. When the cat had kittens, Newton dutifully cut smaller holes next to the big hole—one for each kitten.

Newton had few friends. He constantly quarreled with his colleagues over who had thought of an idea first. An astronomer whose career Newton had nearly destroyed described him as being "insidious, ambitious, excessively covetous of praise, and impatient of contradiction."

NEWTON'S TELESCOPE

In Woolsthorpe and back at Cambridge, Newton experimented with light. He had been inspired to think about the nature of light after seeing a halo around the moon. Light passing through tiny particles of ice suspended high in Earth's atmosphere causes a halo—but Newton didn't know this. Wondering about the cause of the colorful halo led Newton to improve on Galileo's telescope, creating an astronomical instrument of vital importance.

Newton discovered that when white light passes through a prism, it refracts, bending and breaking up into separate colored bands of light. The entire range of bands is called a spectrum. (The word *spectrum* comes from a Latin word meaning "image.")

Newton realized that light does the same thing when it passes through a lens. At that time, almost all telescopes were made with lenses. This kind of telescope is called a refracting telescope. Refracting telescopes of the 1600s had an annoying flaw. Objects viewed through them appeared with fuzzy fringes of color between dark and light areas. This effect, called chromatic aberration, made it hard for astronomers to see details and to accurately measure positions of the stars and planets.

Newton realized that a curved mirror would not cause chromatic aberration and could function as a lens. Light reflects off a mirror, so objects seen through a reflecting telescope (one that uses mirrors instead of lenses) would appear sharp and focused. Several earlier scientists had made this suggestion. But Newton was the first to actually build a reflecting telescope, which is sometimes also called a Newtonian telescope in his honor. In 1671 Newton demonstrated his reflecting telescope to the Royal Society. Their interest eventually encouraged him to publish his notes on the study of light and color.

Newton's research into optics led him to invent an entirely new type of telescope: the refractor. It was not only simpler, but it eliminated many of the faults of the older style. This is a photo of Newton's original model, which is only 6 inches (15 centimeters) long!

THE GLUE THAT BINDS THE SOLAR SYSTEM

In the late 1670s, Newton returned to investigating gravitation. He knew that Kepler had puzzled over the mysterious force that keeps the moon orbiting Earth and the planets circling the sun. Kepler had tried to guess what the force might be. Among other things, he suggested magnetism. At the time, magnetism was the only known force that could act invisibly at a distance.

Newton believed that an entirely different force was at work. This theory came from his work on the law of inertia, the first of Newton's three great laws of motion. This law states that an object at rest will stay at rest unless an outside force acts on it. If an object is moving, it will keep moving at the same speed in a straight line unless something interferes with it. According to the law of inertia, the moon would be flying off into space in a straight line unless something was interfering with it to make it circle Earth.

Newton proposed that the interfering force was gravity. He suggested that it was the same force that pulls a dropped ball to Earth and that keeps Earth in its orbit around the sun and Jupiter's moons in their orbits around that planet. Every object in the solar system, according to Newton, is pulling on every other object.

Newton discovered that the amount of pull an object exerts depends on how much of it there is. He wrote that the gravitational force of all bodies is determined "according to the quantity of solid matter which they contain." So the more mass a body has, the more it pulls on other objects. Everything that has mass creates gravity: the sun, the moon, Earth, and even people.

"**There is a power** of gravity tending to all bodies proportional to the quantity of matter which they contain."

—Isaac Newton, 1687

Gravity, Newton found, is not a very strong force. An object's gravitational pull declines rapidly as the distance from the center of the object increases. Let's say you're standing outside with your feet on the ground. But you have the ability to fly. You fly twice as far from the center of Earth as you would when standing on the ground. Earth's gravitational pull on you declines to one-fourth. If you fly ten times farther from the center of Earth, Earth's gravity pulls on you with only one-hundredth the force it has when you're standing on the ground.

Newton's discovery perfectly explained the motion of the bodies in our solar system. Kepler had noticed that a planet moves slower when it is farther from the sun and faster when it is closer to the sun. Newton explained why. When a planet is farther from the sun, the sun's gravitational pull is weaker. When a planet is close to the sun, the sun's gravitational pull is stronger.

Gravity also explained the shape of planet orbits. The planets might orbit the sun in perfect circles if nothing else affected their orbits. But the planets themselves have gravity. This means that they pull on one another as they circle the sun. This pull is slight compared to the sun's pull, but the effect adds up. Its result is orbits that are ellipses instead of perfect circles.

Altogether, Newton's ideas about gravity make up Newton's law of universal gravitation. Newton said his own law was inspired by Kepler's third law of planetary motion, which says that planets farther from the sun take longer to orbit the sun than do planets closer to the sun.

THE *PRINCIPIA*

Newton gathered all his discoveries about optics, gravity, and more into a single book. He published this book, *Philosophiae naturalis principia mathematica* (Mathematical principles of natural philosophy), or the *Principia* for short, in 1687. Many people believe it is the single greatest work in the history of science. In more than five hundred pages, Newton explains the motions of and relationships among the planets, the sun, and the moon; the dynamics of waves and tides; the concepts of mass, inertia, and motion; and all three of his famous laws of motion.

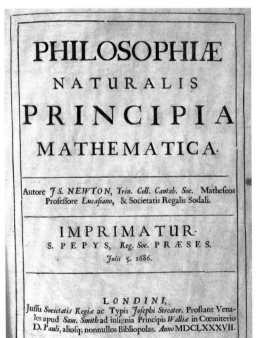

The title page of the *Principia* (1687), Newton's masterpiece. In this one book, Newton laid the foundation for much of modern physics, astronomy, and even space travel.

Newton's three laws of motion say:
1. An object at rest remains at rest unless an outside force acts on it. An object in motion continues in motion at the same speed and in the same direction unless an outside force acts on it. In other words, an object tends to keep doing what it is already doing.
2. When a force acts on an object, it accelerates (changes the speed and direction of) the object. The greater the object's mass is, the greater the force needed to accelerate it is. This means that the heavier an object is, the harder it is to move.
3. For every action, there is an equal and opposite reaction.

The book also states that all "physical bodies are built of atoms." Atoms are the bits of matter that make up molecules. A molecule is

GETTING THERE

Newton's third law of motion states that for every action, there is an equal and opposite reaction. For example, when something moves forward (an action), something else moves backward the same amount (a reaction). Newton's third law eventually led to the giant rockets that propel spacecraft to the moon, Mars, and beyond.

You can see Newton's third law in action for yourself:

Blow up a balloon and then let it go. It flies around the room. Why? The air rushing from the neck of the balloon is an action. The flight of the balloon in the opposite direction is the reaction.

Stand carefully on a skateboard and then jump off it. As you head in one direction (action), the skateboard shoots off in the other (reaction).

Rockets work in a similar way. The hot gases shooting from the rocket motor are an action. This action creates a reaction in the opposite direction, propelling the rocket.

the smallest possible portion of a substance. Everything is made of molecules.

In the *Principia*, Newton consolidated the ideas of Copernicus, Kepler, and Galileo and solved many mysteries and problems that had dogged his predecessors. He showed that nature is one vast machine that follows simple rules. The sun, the planets, their moons, and everything else in the universe are gears in this machine. Newton believed that everything happens for a reason, resulting in a chain of events that can be predicted with mathematical precision. The curve of a cannonball as it flies though the air can be calculated in advance using the same formulas that predict solar eclipses and the paths of comets.

When he published the *Principia*, Newton had provided fundamental definitions of space, time, force, gravitation, inertia, action, and reaction. For the next three centuries, these definitions were the foundation of physics. Newton's colleagues did not universally and immediately accept all the ideas in the *Principia*, however. For example, Christiaan Huygens, a Dutch mathematician, astronomer, and physicist, wrote in 1690, "I am not especially in agreement with a Principle that [Newton] supposes . . . namely, that . . . two or more different bodies attract one another or tend to approach each other mutually . . . the cause of such an attraction is not explicable either by any principle of Mechanics or by the laws of motion."

But by the end of his life, Newton had few detractors. When Newton died in 1727, he was one of the most famous men in all of Europe. For the first time in its history, Great Britain provided a state funeral for a common man—the kind of funeral normally reserved for royalty or great military leaders. He was laid to rest in London's Westminster Abbey, where British royalty and other prominent citizens are buried.

Chapter 6

The New Universe

For many people in the 1500s and the 1600s, believing that Earth is not the center of the universe came at a cost. Copernicus feared for his church career. Giordano Bruno lost his life. Kepler risked his neck supporting Galileo's ideas. Galileo himself spent the last nine years of his life under house arrest. These men faced opposition for a variety of reasons. Heliocentrism seemed to defy visual observation and common sense. Many people also found heliocentrism deeply offensive. They were reluctant to give up their long-cherished position as God's most important creation. In addition, Protestant Christians believed that if the Bible says Earth has corners and the sun and stars circle it, then it must be so.

The Catholic Church had originally been friendly to heliocentrism. But the church faced increasing opposition from different directions. Renaissance thinkers were beginning to defy church teachings and the Protestant Church was growing. To maintain its grip on power, the Catholic Church cracked down on people—such as Bruno and Galileo—who questioned its authority. Newton, unlike his scientific predecessors, faced no religious opposition. Newton published his work in the same century as Galileo. What was different for Newton?

NEWTON'S WORLD

First, Newton lived in England. The Church of England was more flexible than the Protestant and Catholic churches were. The dreaded Inquisition never arrived in England. English scientists and philosophers could discuss their work openly, without fear of religious opposition. Also, a new intellectual era had begun sometime between Galileo and Newton. Thinkers who worked during this era, called the Enlightenment, advocated religious tolerance and democracy. They emphasized the importance of reason and logic. All people, they said, are capable of thinking independently. People should not automatically believe those in power—including church leaders. People should believe only what they discover through their own reasoning. When Copernicus, Kepler, and Galileo worked, true scientific thinkers were rare. Newton, however, worked during an era teeming with scientists.

After more than fifteen hundred years of scientific darkness in Europe, technology was making huge strides there. Invention after invention appeared. The piano, the steam engine, the diving bell, pendulum clocks, ice cream, the barometer, calculating machines, and countless other new items burst onto the scene during Newton's time. Steadily, people became less afraid to ask questions about Earth and its place in the universe or to express doubts about long-held beliefs.

The seventeenth century saw great advances in science and technology. One example is this diving bell, invented by Edmund Halley, of Halley's comet fame. With it, he hoped to recover treasure from sunken ships.

NEWTON AND GOD

Newton was a devoutly religious man. A profound belief in God permeates all of his work. Newton believed that his laws revealed a clockwork universe. He saw the universe as a machine wound up by God at the Creation and allowed to run on its own ever since.

Newton's laws govern all motions in the universe, large and small. The same laws that determine the courses of the stars and planets also control the falling of a leaf from a tree. Newton was certain that if he could measure the mass and motion of a single atom, he could predict its every move for the next million years.

They pointed out that, if Newton's theory was true, once God had set this perfect machine in motion, there would be no further need for God. This critique troubled Newton. So he argued that God was still necessary. "Gravity explains the motions of the planets," he said, "but it cannot explain who set the planets in motion."

ℰNLIGHTENED THINKERS

Some of the great thinkers working around Newton's time included these:

Daniel Bernoulli (1700–1782), who gave us our laws about gas pressure

Anders Celsius (1701–1744), astronomer, and **Daniel Gabriel Fahrenheit** (1686–1736), physicist and engineer, who gave their names to the temperature scales we use in the twenty-first century

René Descartes (1596–1650), philosopher and mathematician, who refined the fields of calculus, geometry, and optics

Pierre Gassendi (1592–1655), priest and astronomer, who tried to reconcile Christianity with scientific reason

Carl Friedrich Gauss (1777–1855), philosopher and mathematician, who developed modern number theory (a branch of mathematics dealing with the properties of numbers)

Edward Jenner (1749–1823), who developed the first vaccines and the technique of vaccination

Pierre-Simon Laplace (1749–1827), a mathematician and astronomer who developed a theory about the origin of the solar system

Antoine Lavoisier (1743–1794), a chemist who discovered oxygen and hydrogen

Blaise Pascal (1623–1662), a mathematician who also invented one of the first calculating machines

Antoni van Leeuwenhoek (1632–1723), inventor of the microscope and discoverer of microbes (microscopic organisms, or living things too small to distinguish with the naked eye)

James Watt (1736–1819), inventor of the first widely used steam engine

Christopher Wren (1632–1723), scientist and architect, who designed and built Saint Paul's Cathedral in London

Newton viewed God as a mechanic who stands back from his work once it's finished. Newton's God doesn't get directly involved with humankind or the daily operation of the universe. This view is called Deism. Newton didn't invent Deism, but his theories made it very popular. Newton's ideas appealed greatly to Enlightenment thinkers. Here, they said, is a universe explained by mathematics, the purest reasoning imaginable.

Newton did not want his laws used to push God to the sidelines. Newton feared that Deism would lead to atheism of which he had a deep-seated horror. So Newton formulated an idea that suggested that as perfect a machine as the universe is, it occasionally needs fine-tuning. Just as a complex machine needs an engineer to keep it well oiled and properly adjusted, the universe needs God to keep a hand in things. The German mathematician Gottfried Leibniz scoffed at this suggestion:

> Sir Isaac Newton and his Followers have also a very odd
> Opinion concerning the Work of God. According to their Doctrine,
> God Almighty wants to wind up his Watch from Time to Time:
> Otherwise it would cease to move. He had not, it seems, sufficient
> Foresight to make it a perpetual Motion. Nay, the Machine of God's
> making, is so imperfect, according to these Gentlemen, that he
> is obliged to clean it now and then . . . and even to mend it, as a
> Clockmaker mends his Work.

Although Newton's religious ideas faced substantial opposition, his scientific ones faced little. By the end of the 1600s, scientists, most educated people, and even many religious leaders accepted the heliocentric theories of Copernicus, Kepler, Galileo, and Newton.

In 1686 French author Bernard Le Bovier de Fontenelle published a book titled *Entretiens sur la pluralité des mondes*

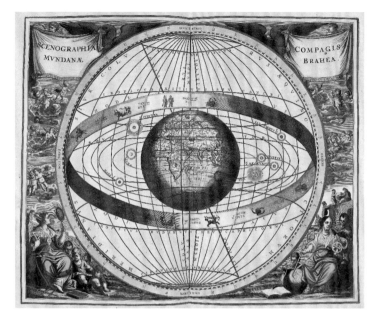

An illustration from 1660 showing Tycho Brahe's vision of the planets and the sun orbiting Earth. By this time, the geocentric model of the universe was already being replaced.

(Conversations on the plurality of the worlds). This book, which explained the Copernican system to ordinary people, was very popular and influential. It declared the following:

> Tycho Brahe, who had fixed the Earth in the Center of the Universe, turned the Sun round the Earth, and the rest of the Planets round the Sun, because new discoveries in astronomy left no way to have the Planets turn round the Earth. But among so many great Planetary bodies how could you exempt the Earth alone from turning round the Sun? It certainly seems improper to make the Sun turn round the Earth, when all the Planets turn round the Sun. Though Brahe's System was invented to maintain the immobility of the Earth, yet it was very improbable. So we resolve to stick to Copernicus, whose Opinion was most Uniform and Probable.

Almost everyone had finally come to agree on this conclusion.

Chapter 7

The Idea That Wouldn't Die

$\mathcal{S}$ince the late 1600s, most scientists, religious leaders, and ordinary people have accepted a heliocentric view of the universe. But geocentrism has never died out completely. For example, a religious sect called the Muggletonians emerged in England in the 1650s. It lasted more than three centuries, until the last Muggletonian died in 1979. The Muggletonians shared some of Newton's religious beliefs, such as that God takes no notice of creation on a daily basis. But Muggletonians rejected Newton's heliocentric cosmology. They believed that the sun and the moon are exactly the size they appear to be in the sky. Founder John Reeve insisted in the Muggletonians' sacred text, "Hearken no more unto vain astronomers or star-gazers, concerning the bulk of the sun, moon and stars, for I positively affirm from the God that made them that the compass of their bodies are not much bigger than they appear to our natural sight." According to the Muggletonians, Earth is very large compared to the other celestial bodies. The tiny sun, moon, and stars are attached to the inner surface of a sphere only 6 miles (9.7 km) above Earth's surface.

In the 1800s and the early 1900s, several religious groups firmly opposed Copernicus, Kepler, Galileo, Newton, and almost all astronomers. Members of these groups believed that Earth lies motionless at the center of the solar system. This belief relied on passages in the Bible. Some of these groups were small sects. Others were large Christian denominations. One of the largest such groups was the Missouri Synod of the Lutheran Church in the United States. It taught geocentrism from 1870 until 1920.

TEED AND VOLIVA

In the 1870s, a U.S. physician and doctor named Cyrus Teed founded a religious sect called the Koreshan Unity. The Koreshan Unity lasted for about one century. Among other things, Teed believed that Earth is a hollow sphere, like a basketball, and that we live on the inside surface of the sphere. This sphere, 8,000 miles (12,875 km) in diameter, contains the entire universe. The sun is just 8 feet (2.4 m) in diameter and lies only 4,000 miles (6,437 km) away, at the exact center of the sphere. We don't see the sun directly, though. All we see is a reflection. The sun is dark on one side and light on the other. Night and day occur as the sun rotates. The moon and planets are only reflections of Earth's crust. The stars are reflections of the sun's light. All astronomical phenomena, such as eclipses, are simply optical illusions.

Teed and his followers tried hard to prove their hollow-Earth theory. To do this, Teed invented a measuring device called a rectilineator. The structure was made of wood, steel, and brass and

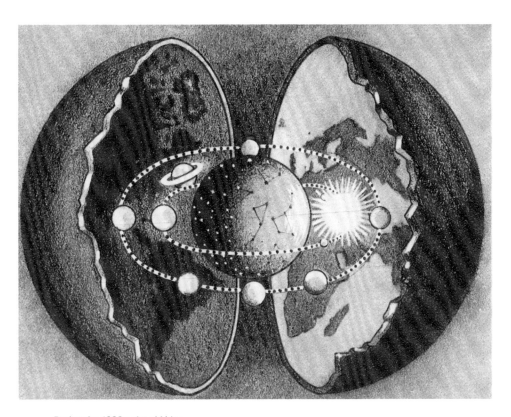

During the 1920s, the old idea that Earth is hollow became very popular in Germany. This illustration of the theory proposed by Karl Neupert appeared in his book *Revolution* (1928). Neupert believed we live on the inside surface of a hollow ball. The stars are on a smaller ball suspended in the center, around which the moon and planets orbit.

was designed to allow people to measure very straight lines across Earth's surface. Teed claimed that it worked and proved his theory true. But no one else ever had any success with the rectilineator.

In the first thirty years of the twentieth century, Wilbur Glenn Voliva ruled an Illinois town of six thousand people. Everyone in the town of Zion was a member of Voliva's Christian Catholic Apostolic Church in Zion. They believed in Voliva's theory that Earth is shaped like a pancake. The North Pole, he said, lies at the center of the pancake, and a wall of ice surrounds the edge. The sun, the stars, and the moon—

which are much closer than astronomers tell us—travel circular paths above Earth's surface. Voliva wrote, "The idea of a sun millions of miles in diameter and 91,000,000 miles [146,450,304 km] away is silly. The sun is only 32 miles [51 km] across and not more than 3,000 miles [4,828 km] from the earth." He also believed that Earth could not possibly rotate. He pointed out that if Earth did rotate, a person could jump into the air for one second and come down 193.7 miles (312 km) from the starting point.

Voliva was sure that he was right and every scientist in the world was wrong. He called them "poor, ignorant, conceited fools" and claimed that he could "whip to smithereens any man in the world in a mental battle. I have never met any professor or student who knew a millionth as much on any subject as I do."

MODERN GEOCENTRISM

In the twenty-first century, as satellites orbit Earth and spacecraft traverse the solar system, some people still cling to geocentrism. They believe that Earth lies motionless at the center of the universe. Everything else orbits Earth. Most of these people are deeply religious. They see heliocentrism as a sin because it directly contradicts the Bible.

A Dutch Canadian educator named Walter van der Kamp founded the Tychonian Society in 1971. This name honored Tycho Brahe's refusal to accept the Copernican theory. Van der Kamp believed that Copernicus was wrong and held that an unmoving Earth must lie at the center of the universe. The sun and the moon orbit Earth once per day. The planets in turn orbit the sun. Around Earth and the sun is a shell containing all the stars. This shell is about 1 trillion miles (1.6 trillion km) away. For years van der Kamp published a journal, the *Bulletin of the Tychonian Society*, filled with articles supporting his beliefs. He declared, "Either biology and astronomy lord it over Scripture, throwing light on it and helping us to understand it better, or Scripture's dicta [statements] rule supreme and give infallible guidance to human theorizing about where we are and whence we come."

Van der Kamp died in 1998, but his organization lives on. It changed its name to the Association for Biblical Astronomy. It publishes books proving that every word in the Bible is literally true and that Tycho's concept of the solar system is correct.

The leading modern proponent of geocentrism is Gerardus Bouw, van der Kamp's successor at the Association for Biblical Astronomy. Unlike most geocentrists, Bouw has a PhD in astronomy. He argues that if the Bible is without error—and it is, he says—then Earth must be immobile at the center of the solar system. Like van der Kamp, Bouw prefers Tycho's system. Other astronomers do not take Bouw's theories seriously.

"Either biology and astronomy lord it over Scripture, throwing light on it and helping us to understand it better, or Scripture's dicta [statements] rule supreme and give infallible guidance to human theorizing about where we are and whence we come."

—*Walter van der Kamp, 1989*

Geocentrists form a very small minority of modern religious believers. Most people of most faiths in the modern world are comfortable with the knowledge that Earth rotates and that it revolves around the sun along with the other planets. For example, in a 1992 speech, Pope John Paul II said:

> The different branches of knowledge call for different methods. Thanks to his intuition as a brilliant physicist and by relying on different arguments, Galileo, who practically invented the experimental method, understood why only the sun could function as the centre of the world, as it was then known, that is to say, as a planetary system. The error of the theologians of the time, when they maintained the centrality of the Earth, was to think that our understanding of the physical world's structure was, in some way, imposed by the literal sense of Sacred Scripture.

Geocentrists from the early humans and ancient Greeks to Reeve, Teed, Voliva, van der Kamp, and Bouw share a common appeal. They all address the human need to feel important in the universe. If Earth lies at the center of the universe and the universe revolves around it, then Earth is the most important body—and human beings are the most important creatures—in the universe.

The discoveries of Copernicus, Kepler, Galileo, and Newton upended our human understanding of the universe. What is more, they showed that Earth is just one planet among many others. Later astronomical discoveries revealed that our solar system is not located in the center of our galaxy and that our galaxy is not in the center of anything either. In addition to the planets in our solar system, astronomers have discovered nearly four hundred planets orbiting other stars.

Epilogue

In 1979, in response to social pressures on the church, Pope John Paul II ordered an in-depth study of the Galileo case. The Vatican (the central government of the Catholic Church) formed a scholarly commission to do just that. The commission studied the case for thirteen years. It presented its report to the pope on October 31, 1992. Among other things, the commission said:

> From the Galileo case we can draw a lesson which is applicable today in analogous cases which arise in our times and which may arise in the future. It often happens that, beyond two partial points of view which are in contrast, there exists a wider view of things which embraces both and integrates them.

Pope John Paul II responded, "Galileo sensed in his scientific research the presence of the Creator who, stirring in the depths of his spirit, stimulated him, anticipating and assisting his intuitions." A few days later, the pope explained that religion and science are different branches of knowledge trying to answer similar questions but through different means. He also clarified that church officials of the 1600s had erred in thinking that humans must accept the Bible's cosmology literally. Eight years later, in 2000, the pope issued a formal apology for all the mistakes committed by some Catholics throughout the church's history, including the trials of the Inquisition. However, the church did not say it had been wrong to silence Galileo. Nor did it specifically apologize for Galileo's condemnation.

The Catholic Church has a complicated relationship with science and scientists. On the one hand, the church has silenced—and even executed—scientists who have contradicted church teachings. On the other hand, the church itself participates in scientific research. Since the late 1500s, for example, the Vatican has been active in astronomical research. And since the late 1700s,

An Honorable Burial

When Nicolaus Copernicus died in 1543, he was buried in an unmarked grave beneath the floor of Frombork Cathedral. In 1616 the Catholic Church listed his book *De revolutionibus* on its *Index Liborum Prohibitorum* (List of Forbidden Books). The book remained banned until 1758. A few decades later, researchers began looking for Copernicus's remains. The researchers finally found him in 2005. They exhumed his remains for study.

On May 24, 2010, Copernicus finally received an honorable burial in a marked grave in Frombork Cathedral. The ceremony took place on the 467th anniversary of his death. A representative of the Catholic Church in Poland expressed regret for the church's condemnation of Copernicus's theory. He criticized the "excesses of the self-proclaimed defenders of the Church" who had condemned Copernicus's work.

The Vatican Observatory is one of the oldest and most respected in the world. Its main observatory is located on the rim of an ancient volcano, not far from Rome. Here, Vatican astronomers do important research on our solar system and the universe.

the church has operated the Vatican Observatory in Italy. This is one of the most respected astronomical organizations in the world. It is famous for its research on the origin of the solar system and the structure of galaxies. In the mid-1800s, the Catholic astronomer Angelo Secchi, working at the Vatican Observatory, was the first to classify stars according to their color. He was also one of the first astronomers to declare that the sun is simply another star. The modern observatory operates in partnership with researchers at the University of Arizona.

In spite of the Vatican's contributions to astronomy, many people still blame the church for its role in silencing Galileo. When this happened, they say, the church hindered scientific progress and public understanding of science. George Coyne thinks this assessment is unfair. Coyne, an astronomer and Catholic priest, was the director of the Vatican Observatory for twenty-eight years. He also cochaired the commission that studied the Galileo case. Coyne said, "The Galileo affair was fabulously interesting, and it did show a degree of ignorance on the part of the church, there's no doubt about that. But to say that that's characteristic of the church's attitude toward science is where I think a big leap is made."

"**The error** of the theologians of the time, when they maintained the centrality of the Earth, was to think that our understanding of the physical world's structure was, in some way, imposed by the literal sense of Sacred Scripture."

—*Pope John Paul II, 1992, referring to Galileo's time*

DIFFERENT ROLES

Most religious leaders and followers have little problem with the discoveries of Newton, Galileo, Kepler, and Copernicus. They feel the Bible and other sacred texts are not meant to teach science. The late American paleontologist Stephen Jay Gould said that science and religion play different roles in our lives. He referred to this difference as "non-overlapping magisteria." Science, Gould said, covers the empirical realm (facts, observations, and experiences). Science concerns itself with what the universe is made of and how it works. Religion covers the spiritual realm. It concerns itself with questions of ultimate meaning and moral value.

The National Academy of Sciences (NAS) agrees with Gould. "Scientists," says NAS, "like many others, are touched with awe at the order and complexity of nature. Indeed, many scientists are deeply religious. But science and religion occupy two separate

THE SCIENTIFIC METHOD

The scientific method includes five basic steps:

1. Observe and describe a phenomenon.
2. Create a hypothesis to explain the phenomenon.
3. Use the hypothesis to predict the existence of other phenomena.
4. Conduct experiments to test the predictions. Experiments must be performed properly and conducted by several independent experimenters.
5. If the experiments support the hypothesis, it may become a theory or a law. If the experiments do not support the hypothesis, it must be rejected or modified.

Scientists often say that theories can never be proved—only disproved. The possibility always exists that some new observation or experiment will conflict with a previously accepted theory.

realms of human experience. Demanding that they be combined detracts from the glory of each."

Coyne suggested that Galileo would agree too. "He said that Scripture is intended to teach us how to go to heaven, and not how the heavens go. It's a beautiful phrase, and it says that Scripture is not teaching science. Scripture is made up of many literary forms: Some of it's poetry, some of it's history, but none of it's science. Galileo really understood that and tried to get others to understand it. He was a better theologian than any of them."

GLOSSARY

alchemy: an ancient philosophic and experimental practice related to the effort to change common substances into pure elements. Many alchemists focused on trying to make a substance that can turn lead into gold and to cure humans of their illnesses.

astrology: the study of celestial bodies to gain information about human affairs. Astrology is a pseudoscience.

astronomy: the scientific study of the universe

chromatic aberration: the visual effect that occurs when a lens breaks up white light into different colors. Objects viewed through the lens appear with fuzzy fringes of color between dark and light areas.

constellation: a group of stars that humans view as a pattern. In ancient times, constellations were thought to influence human behavior and served as practical guides to sailors at sea.

cosmology: a philosophical or scientific view of the structure of the universe

Deism: the belief that God created the universe and then abandoned it, assuming no control over life or influence on natural phenomena

doctrine: an official teaching or position on an issue

ellipse: a flattened circle. A circle has a single center point, while an ellipse has two center points. Each of these is called a focus.

fixed stars: stars that are so distant from Earth that they appear fixed in place, even as Earth moves through space

foci: the two center points of an ellipse

geocentric: Earth-centered

gravity: a force of attraction that exists naturally between all material objects. Isaac Newton developed the idea of gravity as the force responsible for keeping the moon in its orbit around Earth and the planets in their orbits around the sun.

heliocentric: sun-centered

heretic: someone who publicly disagrees with established religious teachings

horoscope: a diagram of the sun, moon, stars, and planets used to predict events in a person's life

hypothesis: a proposed explanation for an observed phenomenon

inertia: the tendency of an object to remain in motion or at rest unless disturbed

law: in science, a generally accepted fact about the physical world

mass: the amount of matter in an object

optics: the study of the behavior and properties of light

orbit: the path of one object around another, such as the path of Earth around the sun

parallax: a change in the apparent position of a nearby object against the backdrop of farther objects, caused by the motion of the observer

pendulum: a freely swinging weight hanging on the end of a cord attached to a fixed support

period: the length of time a celestial body takes to orbit another body, or the length of time it takes a pendulum to complete one cycle—a swing away from and back to its starting position

prism: a solid, transparent object with flat, polished surfaces. When light passes through a prism it refracts, breaking into separate bands of different colors.

pseudoscience: a branch of study that has the appearance of science but does not follow the scientific method. *Pseudoscience* comes from the Greek words for "false science."

radius vector: in astronomy, a line from the center of the sun to the center of a planet

refraction: the bending and breaking up of white light into different-colored bands of light. Refraction occurs when light passes through a lens or prism.

retrograde motion: the apparent reversal of a planet's normal motion against the background of stars

spectrum: the entire range of bands of colored light created when a beam of white light refracts

theory: a hypothesis, or proposed explanation for an observed phenomenon, that has passed some observational and experimental tests

SOURCE NOTES

11 Nevill McMorris, *The Natures of Science*, Cranbury, NJ: Fairleigh Dickinson University Press, (1989), p. 214.

16 "Aristotle," *Today in Science History*, 2009, http://www.todayinsci.com/A/Aristotle/Aristotle-Quotations.htm (January 28, 2013).

16 "Aristotle," *Today in Science History*.

16–17 Michael Fowler, "How the Greeks Used Geometry to Understand the Stars," *Galileo and Einstein*, September 16, 2008, http://galileoandeinstein.physics.virginia.edu/lectures/greek_astro.htm (August 27, 2010).

22 Nicolaus Copernicus, "The Commentariolus: Nicholas Copernicus' Sketch of His Hypotheses for the Heavenly Motion," trans. David Banach, Department of Philosophy, St. Anselm College, n.d., http://dbanach.com/copernicus-commentarilous.htm (December 12, 2012).

22 Institute for the History of Science/Polish Academy of Sciences, "Nicolaus Copernicus Thorunensis," n.d., http://copernicus.torun.pl/en/archives/astronomical/1/?view=transkrypcja&lang=en (January 28, 2013).

24 Nicholas Schonberg, "Letter to Nicolas Copernicus, November 1, 1536," published in "The Text of Nicholas Copernicus: De Revolutionibus (On the Revolutions), 1543 c.e.," available online at *Calendars through the Ages*, 2008, http://www.webexhibits.org/calendars/year-text-Copernicus.html (August 16, 2010).

25 William K. Hartmann, *Astronomy: The Cosmic Journey* (Belmont, CA: Wadsworth, 1985), 113.

25 Ibid.

26 Ibid.

28 Martin Luther, *Tischreden*, quoted in "A Brief Note on Religious Objections to Copernicus," Ohio State University, Department of Astronomy, January 2, 2005, http://www.astronomy.ohio-state.edu/~pogge/Ast161/Unit3/response.html (March 5, 2013).

28 "Psalm 93: New American Standard Bible," *Biblos.com*, n.d., http://www.biblebrowser.com/psalms/93-1.htm (August 16, 2010).

28 "Psalm 104: New American Standard Bible," *Biblos.com*, n.d., http://www.biblebrowser.com/psalms/104-1.htm (August 16, 2010).

32 Carl Sagan, *Cosmos*, New York: Random House Digital, 2011, 45.

33 Max Caspar, *Kepler* (New York: Dover Publications, 1993), 110.

34 Dino Boccaletti, "From the Epicycles of the Greeks to Kepler's Ellipse: The Breakdown of the Circle Paradigm," *Cornell University Library arxiv.org*, June 2001, http://arxiv.org/pdf/physics/0107009 (August 27, 2010).

35–36 Carl Sagan, *Cosmos*, New York: Random House Digital, 2011, 45.

38 James R. Voelkel, *Johannes Kepler and the New Astronomy* (New York: Oxford University Press, 1999), 130.

43 John Desmond Bernal, *A History of Classical Physics* (New York: Barnes & Noble, 1997), 169.

44 Mary Proctor, *The Young Folk's Book of the Heavens* (Boston: Little, Brown, 1930), 30.

45 Buffy Silverman, *Simple Machines: Forces in Action* (Chicago: Heinemann Library, 2009), 25.

45 Steven Kreis, "Galileo, The Starry Messenger (1610)," *The History Guide: Lectures on Modern European Intellectual History*, May 13, 2004, http://www.historyguide .org/intellect/starry.html (August 27, 2010).

45 George Gamow, *Biography of Physics* (New York: Harper & Row, 1961), 47.

45–46 Ibid.

46–47 Ibid., 48.

47 "Genesis 1: New American Standard Bible," *Biblos.com*, n.d., http://nasb .scripturetext.com/genesis/1.htm (August 20, 2010).

47 Dava Sobel, "His Place in Science," *NOVA: Galileo's Battle for the Heavens*, July 2002, http://www.pbs.org/wgbh/nova/galileo/science.html (August 20, 2010).

48 Carl Sagan, *Pale Blue Dot: A Vision of the Human Future in Space* (New York: Random House, 1994), 29.

50 Gamow, *Biography of Physics*, 49.

51 Douglas Linder, "Papal Condemnation (Sentence) of Galileo: June 22, 1633," *Famous Trials*, 2002, http://www.law.umkc.edu/faculty/projects/ftrials/galileo/ condemnation.html (August 20, 2010).

54 Fritz Kahn, *Design of the Universe* (New York: Crown, 1954), p. 14.

54 Gamow, *Biography of Physics*, 53.

57 Kahn, *Design of the Universe*, 14.

59 Ibid., 18.

60 George Smith, "Newton's Philosophiae Naturalis Principia Mathematica," *Stanford Encyclopedia of Philosophy*: Winter 2008 Edition, December 20, 2007, http://plato .stanford.edu/archives/win2008/entries/newton-principia/ (August 25, 2010).

63 John Hudson Tiner, *Exploring the World of Physics: From Simple Machines to Nuclear Energy* (Green Forest, AR: Master Books, 2006), 30.

65 John Bruno Hare, "From the Closed World to the Infinite Universe by Alexandre Koyré," *Internet Sacred Text Archive*, http://sacredtexts.com/astro/cwiu/cwiu14 .htm (August 27, 2010).

67 Glyn Hughes, "The Condensed Edition of Sir Isaac Newton Mathematical Principles of Natural Philosophy," *Glyn Hughes' Squashed Philosophers*, 2009, http://www.btinternet.com/~glynhughes/squashed/newton.htm (August 27, 2010).

66 E. T. Babinski, "Cretinism or Evilution?" *The TalkOrigins Archive*, n.d., http://www.talkorigins.org/faqs/ce/2/part1.html (August 27, 2010).

67-68 John Reeve, *Divine Looking Glass or the Third and Last Testament of Our Lord Jesus Christ* (1661) (Whitefish, MT: Kessinger Publishing, 2003), 31.

70 Martin Gardner, *Fads and Fallacies in the Name of Science* (New York: Dover, 1957), 17.

70 Ibid., 19.

71 Walter van der Kamp, "The Whys and Wherefores of Geocentricity," *The Official Geocentricity Website*, n.d., http://www.geocentricity.com/bibastron/ts_history/history1.html (August 28, 2010).

71 Van der Kamp, "The Whys and Wherefores."

72 Caltech Newman Center, "Faith Can Never Conflict with Reason," *Faith and Science: Catholic Perspectives*, n.d., http://www.its.caltech.edu/~nmcenter/sci-cp/sci-9211.html (August 28, 2010).

73 "Studi Galileiani," *Vatican Observatory*, 2013, http://vaticanobservatory.org/index.php/en/publications/cat-studi-galileiani (March 6, 2013).

73 Bulent Atalay, *Math and the Mona Lisa* (Washington, DC: Smithsonian Institution, 2006), 234.

76 Caltech Newman Center, "Faith Can Never Conflict with Reason," *Faith and Science: Catholic Perspectives*, n.d., http://www.its.caltech.edu/~nmcenter/sci-cp/sci-9211.html (August 28, 2010).

76 Jim Erickson, "The Vatican Observatory Is One of the Oldest Astronomical Institutes in the World," *SPACE.com*, July 16, 2000, http://www.space.com/scienceastronomy/astronomy/vatican_observe_000716.html (August 30, 2010).

76 Stephen Jay Gould, "Nonoverlapping Magisteria," *The Unofficial Stephen Jay Gould Archive*, March 1997, http://www.stephenjaygould.org/library/gould_noma.html (August 30, 2010).

77 National Aeronautics and Space Administration, "Wilkinson Microwave Anisotropy Probe: Frequently Asked Questions," *National Aeronautics and Space Administration*, May 25, 2010, http://map.gsfc.nasa.gov/site/faq.html (August 30, 2010).

77 Erickson, "The Vatican."

74 Agence France-Presse, "Copernicus's Remains Reburied in Polish Cathedral," *Inquirer.net*, May 23, 2010, http://newsinfo.inquirer.net/breakingnews/world/view/20100523-271572/Copernicuss-remains-reburied-in-Polish-cathedral (August 30, 2010).

SELECTED BIBLIOGRAPHY

Campbell, Mary B. *Wonder and Science: Imagining Worlds in Early Modern Europe.* Ithaca, NY: Cornell University Press, 1999.

Couper, Heather, and Nigel Henbest. *The History of Astronomy.* Buffalo: Firefly Books, 2007.

Davis, Joel. *Journey to the Center of Our Galaxy.* Chicago: Contemporary Books, 1991.

Dick, Wolfgang R. "Astronomiae Historia: History of Astronomy." Bonn University Argelander Institute for Astronomy. February 12, 2004. http://www.astro.uni-bonn.de/~pbrosche /map.html (August 31, 2010).

Evans, James. *The History and Practice of Ancient Astronomy.* New York: Oxford University Press, 1998.

Ferguson, Kitty. *Tycho and Kepler: The Unlikely Partnership That Forever Changed Our Understanding of the Heavens.* New York: Walker and Company, 2002.

Faure, Gunter, and Teresa M. Mensing. *Introduction to Planetary Science: The Geological Perspective.* Dordrecht, Netherlands: Springer, 2007.

Finocchiaro, Maurice. *The Essential Galileo.* Indianapolis: Hackett, 2008.

Firsoff, V. A. *Our Neighbor Worlds.* New York: Philosophical Library, 1953.

Fowler, Michael. "Galileo and Enstein: Overview and Lecture List." University of Virginia Department of Physics. N.d. http://galileoandeinstein.physics.virginia.edu/lectures /lecturelist.html (August 31, 2010).

Frazier, Kendrick. *Solar System.* Alexandria, VA: Time-Life Books, 1985.

Gamow, George. *Biography of Physics.* New York: Harper and Row, 1961.

Gardner, Martin. *Fads and Fallacies in the Name of Science.* New York: Dover, 1957.

Gleick, James. *Isaac Newton.* New York: Pantheon, 2003.

Hartmann, William K. *Moons and Planets.* Belmont, CA: Wadsworth, 1999.

Hartmann, William K., and Chris Impey. *Astronomy: The Cosmic Journey.* Belmont, CA: Wadsworth, 1985.

Kuhn, Thomas S. *The Copernican Revolution.* Cambridge, MA: Harvard University Press, 1992.

North, John. *Cosmos: An Illustrated History of Astronomy and Cosmology.* Chicago: University of Chicago Press, 2008.

Sagan, Carl. *Cosmos.* New York: Random House, 1980.

———. *Pale Blue Dot: A Vision of the Human Future in Space.* New York: Random House, 1994.

Shermer, Michael. *How We Believe: The Search for God in an Age of Science.* New York: W. H. Freeman, 1999.

Simanek, Donald E. "The Flat Earth." Lock Haven University. 2006. http://www.lhup .edu/~dsimanek/flat/flateart.htm (August 31, 2010).

Singer, Charles. *A Short History of Scientific Ideas to 1900.* Oxford: Oxford University Press, 1977.

Van Helden, Albert. "The Galileo Project." Rice University. N.d. http://galileo.rice.edu (August 31, 2010).

FURTHER INFORMATION

Books

Christianson, Gale E. *Isaac Newton and the Scientific Revolution*. New York: Oxford University Press, 1996.

Fisher, Leonard Everett. *Galileo*. New York: Atheneum, 1992.

Gingerich, Owen, and James MacLachlan. *Nicolaus Copernicus: Making the Earth a Planet*. New York: Oxford University Press, 2005.

Hansen, Rosanna. *Seven Wonders of the Sun and Other Stars*. Minneapolis: Twenty-First Century Books, 2011.

Ingram, Scott. *Nicolaus Copernicus: Father of Modern Astronomy*. Farmington Hills, MI: Blackbirch Press, 2004.

MacLachlan, James. *Galileo Galilei: First Physicist*. New York: Oxford University Press, 1997.

Miller, Ron. *Seven Wonders of the Gas Giants and Their Moons*. Minneapolis: Twenty-First Century Books, 2011.

———. *Seven Wonders of the Rocky Planets and Their Moons*. Minneapolis: Twenty-First Century Books, 2011.

Silverstein, Alvin, Virginia Silverstein, and Laura Silverstein Nunn. *Forces and Motion*. Minneapolis: Twenty-First Century Books, 2009.

———. *The Universe*. Minneapolis: Twenty-First Century Books, 2009.

Sobel, Dava. *Galileo's Daughter: A Historical Memoir of Science, Faith and Love*. New York: Walker & Co., 2011.

Somervill, Barbara A. *Nicolaus Copernicus: Father of Modern Astronomy*. Minneapolis: Compass Point Books, 2005.

White, Michael. *Isaac Newton: Discovering Laws That Govern the Universe*. Farmington Hills, MI: Blackbirch Press, 1999.

Websites

Astronomy

http://www.astronomy.com
This website of *Astronomy* magazine helps visitors find out what it's like on other planets. Learn how far away the stars are. See cool photos and learn to be a skilled skywatcher.

Geocentricity

http://www.geocentricity.com
The official website of the Association for Biblical Astronomy is a good way to learn more about the association's view of the relationship between the Bible and astronomy.

National Aeronautics and Space Administration (NASA)

http://www.nasa.gov
NASA's website is a perfect stop for images, videos, and interactive features from America's space agency. Get the latest updates on NASA missions and much more.

Nine Planets

http://www.nineplanets.org
This website offers an overview of the history, mythology, and current scientific knowledge of the planets, moons, and other objects in our solar system. Photos and an interactive tour of the solar system are part of the site's learning experience.

INDEX

ABOUT THE AUTHOR

Hugo Award-winning author and illustrator Ron Miller specializes in books about science. Among his many titles, he has written *Is the End of the World Near?* and *Special Effects: An Introduction to Movie Magic.* His favorite subjects are space and astronomy. A postage stamp he created is currently on board a spaceship headed for Pluto. His original paintings can be found in collections all over the world. Miller lives in the state of Virginia.

PHOTO ACKNOWLEDGMENTS

The images in this book are used with the permission of: NASA Images, (starfield background) © Ann Ronan Picture Library/Heritage Images, p. 6; Courtesy of Ron Miller, pp. 9, 10, 18, 51 (bottom); © Interfoto/Alamy, p. 13; © Ken Gillham/Robert Harding World Imagery/CORBIS, p. 21 (top); © Bettmann/CORBIS, p. 21 (bottom); © Forum/UIG/Getty Images, p. 23; © Science Source, p. 30; Stephen A. Schwarzman Building/Rare Books Division, The New York Public Library, Astor, Lenox and Tilden Foundations, p. 31 (left); © SSPL/Getty Images, p. 31 (right); © Universal Historical Archive/UIG/Getty Images, p. 35; © Jay Pasachoff/Science Faction/SuperStock, p. 38; © Andrew Duke/Alamy, p. 41 (inset); Xray: NASA/CXC/SAO/D.Patnaude, Optical: DDS, p. 41 (bottom); © Science and Society/SuperStock, pp. 43, 58; © Fine Art Images/SuperStock, p. 46; © Dea Picture Library/De Agostini/Getty Images, p. 49; © Image Asset Management Ltd./SuperStock, p. 56; The Granger Collection, New York, p. 63; © DeAgostini/SuperStock, p. 66; © Mary Evans Picture Library/Alamy, p. 69; © Eric Vandeville/Gamma-Rapho via Getty Images, p. 75.

Front cover: © Eugene Ivanov/Shutterstock.com.

Back cover: NASA Images.

Jacket flaps: NASA Images.